FIT BUSINESS GUIDE
The Workout Plan For Your Brand

BY JAMES PATRICK

ISBN-13: 978-0692191958
ISBN-10: 069219195X

CHAPTER 01: THE IDEA

"Ideas are easy. Implementation is hard." – *Guy Kawasaki*

THE TRUE VALUE OF IDEAS

Every business ever formed started the exact same way: with someone saying, "I have an idea."

The car you got into this morning started with an idea. The coffee you drank this morning started with an idea. Even the book you are reading this on started with an idea.

I have an idea and here is the problem that my idea solves.

In the new highly connected landscape of our economy, there exists a problem with ideas.

That problem is we are inundated and overrun with everyone's ideas and we are simply exhausted hearing about them!

It feels like anyone you talk to has an idea for something.
> *I have an idea for an e-book I want to write.*
> *I have an idea for an online program I want to launch.*
> *I have an idea for a movie I want to film.*
> *I have an idea for a podcast I want to launch.*
> *I have an idea for a mastermind I want to start.*
> *I have an idea for an app I want to create.*

All we hear are people's ideas over and over again to the point we simply start to tune them out. It gets exponentially more frustrating when people are paranoid about the security and sanctity of their ideas.

A few years ago while in the middle of a workout (when I do my best thinking) I came up with an interesting concept for interactive online gaming.

Like many of us do, I ran it by a friend who immediately begged and pleaded with me not to Google it to see if it existed. Why?

He legitimately feared that if I typed it into Google, the search engine would somehow steal the idea and find a way to create and implement it on its own. The irony of the entire situation was that it was not even an idea I wanted to actually do.

Avoiding that paranoid obsession with ideas is the same reason that I almost never sign a NDA (non-disclosure agreement) when I do consulting with entrepreneurs.

I don't sign NDAs because as original as everyone truly believes their idea is, it probably isn't that entirely unique. In the numerous times someone requested I sign an NDA and I declined but they told me their idea anyway, I had heard something similar before.

The harsh reality is that in today's market, ideas standing on their own are worth absolutely nothing.

GIVING YOUR IDEA A PURPOSE

Let's pause right here for a moment. You bought this book looking to launch your idea for a fitness brand into a reality and here I am telling you that your idea isn't worth anything within the first few paragraphs.

I imagine that was not the motivation you were looking for when you opened up your wallet to get this guide – but bear with me as I explain.

The key phrase I used was "ideas *standing on their own* are worth absolutely nothing."

However, an idea coupled with a purpose is worth listening to, worth noticing, worth paying attention to and worth investing in.

What gives an idea purpose? Taking action. The ability to take action shows that you are committed enough to go beyond conceptualization. It shows that you are dedicated enough to your idea to put your name on it. Taking action turns ideas into something validated, something real, and something that can enter the marketplace.

An idea for a blog gets no readers.
An idea for a movie gets no viewers.
An idea for a new app gets no users.
An idea for a new podcast gets no subscribers.

Conversely, a blog that is published can get readers. A movie that is produced can get viewers. An app that gets launched can get users. A podcast that is released can get subscribers.

Earlier I wrote that no one is interested in ideas any longer, and I will stand by that statement. What we are interested in are people who take action on ideas. That is what we want to hear more about. That is what we want to pay attention to, subscribe to, like, follow, support and eventually become customers of.

Fit Business Guide is about moving past the idea stage and pushing you towards entering the marketplace. I am truly excited for your upcoming journey as you launch your idea into a reality.

TAKE A DEEP BREATH AND PREPARE FOR EVERYTHING TO CHANGE

When you give your idea a purpose by putting action behind it to make it a reality – everything will change. Your life will change. How you see the world around you will change. Your relationships will change. Your confidence level will change. How you handle challenges, obstacles and stress will change. Even how you think will change – as action is a magnet for growth.

A massive chasm will forever separate the timeline of your life. On one side of the divide will be your life before you launched and on the other side will be your new life after you made the decision to take action.

That very important line will showcase to the world that you have the ability to make things happen - that you are not just another person with an idea but that you are the person who turns ideas into reality.

What you are going to learn early in this journey is that there is not a specific roadmap to guide you through every single step to take. Even if there existed such a map, it would not be worth following as your path will be as unique to you as your own fingerprint.

This e-book is written to help you through the major milestones in your journey. The decisions you make along the way are yours and yours alone. My intention is to provide you with as much information and guidance as possible to keep you moving in the direction of your choosing. By the end of reading this I want you to have both the strategy to grow your fitness brand as well as the tactics you want to take to achieve your goals. To achieve this we will look at the formation and growth of your idea in both the macro and the micro.

Yet, before I ask you to put your foot on the gas I want you to take a quick moment to close your eyes. Well, first finish reading this section and then close your eyes. I would like you to forecast how your life will be different after reading this book and following the guideposts to turn your idea into a reality. Imagine that in just a few weeks or a few months that your idea is now a reality and that your brand is now in the marketplace.

Imagine how your life will be different. Imagine how you will feel. Imagine what your days will be like. Imagine the lives you will change. Imagine the dent you will make in the universe.

Be very specific in your thoughts. What will your life be like? What will your mornings look like? How will you go through your day? How will your impact reach others? This is a fantastic thing to start to journal on to set your intentions towards moving forward.

WHAT YOU NEED TO GET STARTED
If you think you need a degree in business, you don't. If you think you need lots of money, you don't. If you think you need an extra hundred hours a week, you don't. If you think you need a wealth of experience in starting businesses, you don't.

All you need to do this is the willingness to act. The only way to launch your idea, to bring your brand to market, is by doing.

You are no longer just a personal trainer, or a coach, or a gym owner, or a clothing designer, or a photographer, or a competitor, or a model. You are an entrepreneur.

Say it out loud: *"I am an entrepreneur."*

I love entrepreneurs, and not just because I am in the business of coaching them. I love entrepreneurs because they are, you are, the heroes of our economy.

You represent the future of business and the trends that large corporations will try to emulate and follow.

The difference between an amateur and an entrepreneur is that an entrepreneur does not classify their idea as a hobby. The entrepreneur is willing to take action. The entrepreneur is going to show up and do the work. The entrepreneur will not hide behind the concept of waiting and working something so it can be "perfect." The entrepreneur is willing to overcome the barriers that prevented them from launching before.

Unlike ever before in history, the entrepreneur, solopreneur and small business owner has a significant advantage over larger companies. Not only has the internet become the great equalizer to level the playing field for all, but entrepreneurs have the unique ability to launch faster with more agility while rivaling and surpassing the level of impact, connection and engagement that a larger brand could ever hope to muster up. With the phone in your pocket right now you can literally reach just about anyone in our connected world to form a bond.

The unique advantage that you possess over every large brand is yourself. As you will learn throughout this book, you are the essential human element to your idea that consumers are desperately seeking.

The best time to take action on your idea has already passed, so the next best time is right now. Make the choice and commitment to move forward. Commit right now to taking action.

QUALIFY OR REFINE YOUR IDEA

Not all ideas are equal. We are capable of having both brilliant ideas and brilliantly bad ideas. Some of our ideas are just worth more than others. Your job is to triage to determine which ideas are worthy of your attention and investment and which ideas need to be either refined or abandoned. What follows are a series of questions that you should be asking yourself about your idea so as to either qualify it or revise it before moving forward.

First, what problem does your idea solve? Successful ideas start with finding the right problem to solve. It has to be a problem that people want to have solved. What is the problem people have and how is your idea the right solution to their problem?

Specific to the fitness industry, there is a nearly endless stream of problems that you could set out to try and solve with your idea. People have problems with losing weight, with gaining muscle, with understanding their form and technique, with knowing what to eat, with knowing how to prepare their food, with not having time to prep their meals, with not having access to a gym, with not being able to memorize their workout routines, with not knowing what food is acceptable to eat while traveling, with not understanding how to read labels, with not seeing the results they want from readily available resources, with not having the commitment to follow through on their goals, with finding the right plan for their body type, blood type, gender, background, and so on.

Spend the time to think about your idea with specificity and the problem your idea helps alleviate or solves.

Another way to think about problem solving is to ask yourself what change are you trying to enact. Are you making someone's life easier, better, healthier, happier, less stressful, less fearful, more joyful? For example, you could be developing a clothing line for all the various body types that help women of any shape or size feel amazing and empowered when they walk into the gym. What gift is your idea giving them? Is it more time, more confidence or perhaps better health?

Be careful; at this stage, it is tempting to want to try and solve too many problems at once, essentially scaling your idea bigger than it can be managed at the start. You can create an idea so large that it literally can never take off – and it can be a clever way your fear prevents you from ever starting.

We have all been guilty of this. Suppose you have an idea for an e-mail newsletter to assist women who are pregnant for the first time stay healthy during their term. You sit down to flush out the concept but before you know it, by the time you look at your notes you now have a full blown database website with membership portal for first time pregnancies, to moms with multiple kids to even just women without kids who want to learn about being fit and want to check out your site which would be hosting videos, interviews, podcasts, articles and downloadable modules to follow.

Frustrated and overwhelmed that it is just too much to do and manage, you stop right there. Consider how many genius ideas were abandoned because the inventor over-complicated it.

Do not be afraid to allow your idea to be very specific. Focus on the benefit your idea has for individuals who are dealing with the problem you want to solve. You can't, and don't even want to, be everything for everyone.

The approach is to start small and niche as opposed to trying to be a one-stop shop. When I launched my photography business I made the mistake of trying to provide all types of services to all types of clients. I photographed architecture, events, families, fashion, portraiture, sports and more. On top of that I also offered my clients my experience in graphic design, web strategy and analytics, videography and professional service marketing. Sure, I was a Jack-of-all-trades, but I was known for nothing specific. In fact, clients were often confused by what I even did. The result was I could not keep up with all I was trying to do and ended up losing business as a result. The true growth in my business was when I eliminated everything except for the one thing I was offering. In this case it was unique portraiture of athletic subjects.

If you have a hard time explaining what your idea is and what problem it solves, chances are it probably won't work. So work your idea into a clear and concise concept. Distill it into a single sentence such as: I provide _service_ to _demographic_ to fix _problem_.

Use this as a metric for your brand. If you cannot sum up your idea into a single sentence, you need to distill it down more.

Now you may have looked up my website or the various brands that I manage and be saying, "*Wait just a stinkin' minute there James! I see that you manage a design company offering graphic and web work, you do marketing and brand consulting, public speaking, you wrote this book and several others, you host events and more.*" And you would be right to notice those things. However, the only reason I am able to manage all of those things is because I started small and niche with one idea. Later in this book I will address what scaling looks like and how to do it effectively.

Another warning: saying "I want/need to make money" is not a good problem to solve. Your idea has to be focused on the user. How are you helping or serving consumers? How can you blend together your loves and strengths in the service of others?

Recently I got involved in a mastermind group of various entrepreneurs looking to level up their influence and clout. A significant number of the participants set out to start their own coaching practices or mastermind groups with the intention of increasing their profits without any focus on how they could help others or why they should be helping others.

Without the purity in their purpose and focus on solving a problem, my guess is that most will not succeed.

Secondly, it is important that you want your idea to be different and unique from what is already out in the marketplace, i.e. the better version of the mousetrap. If you are not willing to think or do differently, then you are not actually changing anything and if you are not changing anything it will be hard to notice you in the crowd. Why would anyone hire you if you are offering the exact same thing as something else that already exists in the marketplace?

We as consumers (and really as humans) have programmed ourselves to only notice what is different or unique. As we scroll through Instagram we pause over things that are different and catch our attention. As we fast forward on our DVR we hit play once we see something that disrupts us that we were not expecting to see.

Suppose you are working on an online training guide. What makes your guide unique, different and thus special to your audience? Does it offer something that other online training guides do not? Perhaps it achieves the same results in less time. Perhaps it has an incentive or bonus benefit that others do not. Perhaps it is for a certain group of people that have not yet been targeted or helped.

It is perfectly acceptable to see what others are doing to learn from them and figure out how to differentiate yourself. Your idea could play off something that already exists in the marketplace with a unique spin that makes it your own.

Thirdly, is your idea realistic, doable and attainable? Could you actually make money from your idea and if so, how?

My idea to create an online gaming platform was nothing more than a fun idea that I hope already existed in the marketplace. I had neither the time nor technical competency to make it happen myself. And if I were being honest, I wouldn't have the interest either.

However my idea to write an online training program for entrepreneurs was very realistic as was my idea to develop the FITposium conference, our online education network, my podcast, my blog, my past e-books and my photography and creative agency businesses.

Do the research on your idea to find out what the requirements are to launch. What could be the projected costs, potential roadblocks, technical needs and more?

The final question, which honestly is the most important question: Is this an idea you actually want to do?

Moving forward, you are going to be giving a lot of yourself to make this idea a reality. You have to love it. You have to be obsessed with it. No one can love your idea, your brand, more than you do. You have to be Evangelist Numero Uno!

NEED AN IDEA?

Perhaps you are stuck and looking for an idea you want to move forward with. Here is an idea I got from Daniel H. Pink's book *The Adventures of Johnny Bunko*. Start by compiling a list of everything you feel you are good at doing. Then develop a similar list of things you love to do. See where those two lists overlap by circling things that appear on both. There are naturally things you are good at doing that you don't love and things you love doing but are not good at. But what are the things you both love doing and are good at doing?

Once you have that shortened list you will now factor in a third list. The third list is what people around you need. Your idea will be the overlap of what you're good at doing, what you love to do and what people around you need.

I love helping other people by educating them and I have a long history of successfully helping others through teaching classes, presenting, blogging, podcasting and more. I thus felt it was my responsibility to help share my insights and experience so that others can succeed in their careers. That is your Venn diagram for your life. Find your overlap.

EXERCISE: YOUR FUTURE SELF

Free write your bio of what your life will be like once you launch. What will your life look like? How will it be different? Write in as much detail as you can about how you will feel once your idea is out on the market.

CHAPTER 02: OBTACLES, ROADBLOCKS AND FEARS... OH MY!

"Excuses are a great mechanism to apply logic to our fears." – Mike Michalowicz

DECONSTRUCTING FEAR
Amateurs are scared. That should not come as a surprise to you. They are scared to take risks. They are scared to move forward with their goals. They are scared to move from the comfort of what they know into the realm of what remains unknown.

But what may be a surprise to you is that professionals are just as scared.

Those ridiculous platitudes like "No Fear" are as antiquated as the 90s shirts they were printed on. Anyone that tells you they faced no fear in launching their idea is either lying to you or a robot – in which case you should probably start running away from them.

Fear is the common denominator amongst anyone who has an idea to do something. And regardless of who you are, it always feels the same.

It is important to note that fear means there is some form of risk involved – and if your idea is worth doing it will have risk associated. It is about the need for us to get comfortable with being uncomfortable.

How many times has fear held you back previously? How many times have you made up excuses to not be on the hook for something, or to not be held accountable or to convince yourself it was not a good idea after all?

What, specifically, are we afraid of? We fear that our idea might be too soon, too late, too risky, too boring, too offensive, too complicated, have too many legal issues, is too difficult, too much work, that we might not have enough time, that it has never been done, that is has already been done, that people will ignore it, that people will hate it, that it might fail.

Going a step further... what is at the root of all of these fears? If we dig down deep enough, and we should, all our fears stem from one central worry.

What if people see me as not being good enough?

We become paralyzed with fear thinking that someone is going to think we are not qualified enough, worthy enough, talented enough, whatever-enough to accomplish our idea. And that fear grows, exponentially, out of control. It is called the "imposter syndrome."

It does not matter what our background is, how competent we are, how qualified we are, how great our idea is, how hard we are willing to work – the fear of someone calling us a fraud is crippling.

However, the primary difference between amateurs and professionals is that amateurs allow the fear to stop them whereas professionals will find a way to push past it.

I am not going to throw some useless diatribe on how you need to be courageous and push forward. Tell me something I don't know, right? Besides, that is not how it works anyway!

The courage to overcome things that are very difficult does not come from reading this book. Just as it does not come from blindly and ignorantly ignoring fear like those old mottos recommend.

Courage comes, exclusively, from actually starting the work. That is such a crucial concept that it bears reading a second time. Go ahead, I'll wait.

It can be so small and incremental to start. I did not start my career as a public speaker by traveling coast to coast in the United States speaking to audiences in the size of hundreds. I started by frightfully hiding behind a podium to give a lecture to a college class of 20 students. But after doing that for a while I worked up to getting out from behind the podium, to speaking a little more in front of a slightly bigger group and up and up and up it went.

The more you face the idea of failure, the more you get comfortable with pushing your level of comfort even further – because each time you realize that despite all the anxiety and fear, it did not kill you. In fact, it didn't even hurt you.

I had a co-worker about a decade ago who called this technique "fringing."

Over time you push your boundaries and limitations slowly and incrementally as you fringe further and further out from your comfort zone.

It does not happen with the snap of a finger and you won't really notice any significant changes in the short term. But after you fringe long enough, you will look back at yourself in hindsight and realize you've changed.

Before your first blog article you might be terrified to hit that publish button and maybe as a result you only blog once a month to start. But eventually you start to work yourself up to once every other week and then once a week until blogging does not become a life or death decision. It is just something you do every week.

Anxiety and fear is just the anticipation of a potential future pain. By accomplishing something, even if just small at first, you realize that there is not much pain at the end of the road.

Like any muscle, the more you exercise it, the stronger it gets. The ability to face adversity, fear and obstacles improves the more one does it. What is required upfront is not the strength to overcome any obstacle; it is the willingness to fail. That is what makes us stronger.

CATCHING YOUR FEARS AND PRACTICALLY DESTROYING THEM

What possibly could be more important than pursuing your goals, dreams and ideas? Do you honestly think it is more important to hide from them out of fear? It is essentially to catch your fears before you start to enter into that anxiety spiral.

You cannot worry that your product, service or brand idea will not be good enough and here is the practical reason of why. The reality is that we have a scarcity of things not launching. That is why no one cares about your idea. They only care if you launch it.

The best way to catch your fears and work to overcome those barriers is to physically write them all down. Take out a pen and paper and record every fear you are facing right now, which can (and often does) include self-sabotage. Then next to each of those obstacles, write out three solutions on how you will overcome it.

For example, I have a fear that people might not like this book.

Solution A: Repeat to myself that I have more than 15 years of experience in this industry and I have a lot of valuable information to share.

Solution B: Remind myself that I have successfully applied these lessons through my blogs, podcasts, FITposium conference and Launch Program and have received hundreds, if not thousands, of letters of support and thanks.

Solution C: I will have this book edited by several colleagues I respect for their professional input before I get it published.

To look at fears in this manner, where you can easily and pragmatically find multiple solutions to each, takes most of the power they wield over you.

ONE TERRIFYING QUESTION
When people ask you what do you do – what is your answer? For years while I was growing my photography business and still working in marketing, when people asked me what I did I would tell them I worked in marketing. I would hide my interest in my future career in photography.

What if they judged me for being a photographer?
What if they thought I wasn't good enough to be a photographer?
(Guessing this might sound familiar to you).

It was not until I was far more comfortable with that individual and trusted they would not judge me that I would work into the conversation that I also wanted to be a photographer.

It took me a long time before I could answer that I was a photographer first. But the very moment I did that, everything changed. How I looked at my work changed. How I looked at my goals changed. How I looked at the world around me changed.

Saying or claiming you do something (or want to do something) makes you accountable for it. It puts you on the hook.

That is what makes people uncomfortable. Being on the hook. If you're on the hook to do it then you're expected to do it and that means you could fail. It is just easier to call it a hobby, to not be held accountable for it, to not be judged for it.

But, once again, let's look at the fear practically. Consider public speaking. Most of us are pretty good at talking if we are talking to a close friend or a family member. However when we are asked to stand up in front of a group of people and give a presentation we break out in a cold sweat. We feel terrified. We tell ourselves, *"I can't get up in front of a group of people. They might judge me."*

The same thing happens when you're watching someone else give a presentation and the speaker calls to the audience and you think in your mind, *"Please don't call on me! What if I say something embarrassing or don't know what to ask or say?"*

The brain (well, at least the amygdala portion) triggers these fears to try to keep you safe. It is what triggers when you have to run from a stray dog chasing you. It is what triggers when someone swings his or her fist at you.

But we don't need to be kept safe from being called on during a presentation we are attending, or from publishing a blog of our own or from answering that one question about what we do or want to do for a living. These are not real dangers.
If they were real dangers, there would legitimately be something bad that could happen. But what is the worst thing that could happen?

Imagine you see someone at a party you want to talk to. The brain immediately conjures up a fear, or series of fears, to prevent you from talking to a stranger. Subconsciously we worry that the person is going to slap us in the face and make a public mockery of us. However, unless you are insanely creepy, weird or wacko how legitimate is that fear? What universe does that fear reside in?

The worst thing that could really happen is that they would not be interested in talking to you and the conversation would end. That's all!

Imagine all the fears that come up throughout the course of your day. Fears that come up when someone calls you, when a certain e-mail hits your inbox, when you're asked to give an update to the entire office, when you're asked to post on the company's blog, when you want to go talk to someone you've never met before.

Now, imagine that every time a fear began to surface you paused to ask yourself, *"What is the worst thing that could happen right now?"* What you will find out is that your biggest fears are not even close to as bad as what our subconscious wants us to believe. Doing this makes it significantly easier to do things that at first seemed so difficult and impossible.

Take, for example, the fear of leaving a job to start your own business. What if it doesn't work? What if I fail miserably? Then what?

If that really happened, if the worst came true, then you would just have to get another job until you figured it out again. That is not that bad of a scenario. And if that is the worst thing that could happen, what possibly is stopping you?

That is the exact conversation I had with myself when I was considering leaving my marketing job to work full-time as a photographer. The prospect of it was terrifying until I realized that the worst thing that would happen is I would just have to end up getting a different job in marketing if it all didn't work out. That was much less daunting of a scenario.

It might surprise anyone who knows me, or has seen me present on stage, but I am actually extremely introverted. I am not shy, that is something altogether different. But being around groups of people can be severely draining to my energy and if I had the choice, I would much prefer a quiet evening at home with my puppy. However, I have trained and adapted myself to get more comfortable being around groups of people in order to help reach my goals.

AVOIDING PERFECTION

Fear can also derail or delay a project or idea already in the works. The fear of the project not being ready to put out to the world, of not being perfect can forever stall out launching until you run out of time or money and have to cancel it altogether. Seth Godin calls this "thrashing" and it has impacted many of us to some degree.

Here is an example of how the perfection mentality can destroy your idea. Suppose you want to write an e-book (what I am doing right now in a coffee shop as I listen to Muse blasting through my headphones) and you get to about 80% completion. Then you realize you forgot a whole other section that should be included, so you start working on that.

Once you do that you then realize there were two other people you probably should interview so you set off to do that. Then you feel that you didn't like the design of the e-book so you and your designer begin to redesign everything for scratch. You could literally do this forever – and many have until they eventually give up on the project.

How do you get yourself past the perfection mentality? Seth Godin recommends that you thrash first thing. By this he means that you need to come up with every objection, iteration, concept, audible and end around you can at the start and then figure out ways to push through them all.

When I worked in marketing, we would have to ship out proposals to clients to pursue public sector contracts. A proposal on average would take a few weeks up to a month to create. However, the project manager for the proposal would always show up towards the end of the process. They would casually stroll into the room and make a laundry list of changes and reiterations they wanted to see done with the proposal.

Unfortunately these were all things we, the marketing team, needed to know when we started the process several weeks earlier. By the time they came in to thrash it was too late to effectively make the changes they wanted. We would either miss the client deadline or enact the changes poorly in a rush and end up losing our bid.

Having to deal with this consistently for years, I worked to set a new mandate for marketing campaigns at our office. If project managers wanted their opinions heard, if they wanted to be involved in the proposal effort – then it was required for them to show up at the beginning. Show up at the start and provide all the input, ideas, objections and concepts they wanted to see when we had the time to do it and test it. That was not an unrealistic request.

SUCK FIRST, THEN SUCK LESS
You have to be willing to suck, at least at first. Then, after the idea is launched, you figure out ways to suck a little less.

You have to publish that first sucky blog article or post that first sucky YouTube video or hit print on that first sucky book. You need to launch before you think you are ready.

The problem is not that we have too much sucky content in the market. The problem is we don't have enough willing to get to the market.

The first podcast I recorded was not that good (some may argue that they still are not). The first blogs I posted were not that impressive. The first time I got up to present in front of a group of people was not a film-worthy moment.

But the more I pushed past the suck and launched, the better my content got.

People will forgive efforts; they will forgive updates and revisions as long as you bring it to the marketplace. Consider how many apps you have on your phone and how often those apps have to be updated to improve the user experience or to correct bugs. What you want to launch is no different.

FROM WRITER'S BLOCK TO BEST-SELLING AUTHOR

In 2017 Lindsey Schwartz released her book Powerhouse Woman and it quickly rose to become an Amazon Best Seller. However, looking back on the process, there were moments it almost did not happen.

"I dealt with extreme writer's block," Schwartz said. "Insecurities and huge fears came up. The thought of someone actually reading it became the scariest thing in the world. Putting anything we're creating out into the world. I was scared out of my mind – but here we go."

To overcome her fears and push forward with writing her book, Schwartz would refer back to the client avatar she created (will cover later in this book) and reminded herself that she was writing this book to help that person. That kept her on track.

"Coming back to who I was trying to make a different for helped," Schwartz said. "Trusting that if I had this inspiration and inspiration inside of me that there was someone else out there who needed it. It was not about me."

Thus every day she would sit down to write, even if it was only for 15 minutes and even if it was absolutely awful.

"Your mind does not really want to do hard work; it wants to do easy work. Writer's block is our comfort zone saying, 'Hey, come over here and hang out for a while,'" Schwartz said.

But every day she would continue to force herself past that fear and overcome the writer's block by writing. Of course there were days she could not write a word past 15 minutes and there were days that she ended up throwing out everything she wrote. However, continue to write she did. The more she did it, the more she would have days where she would instead write 2 hours of great content.

Continually referring back to her avatar to guide her, the book was released and did receive the best seller ranking.

EXERCISE: OVERCOMING THE IMPOSTER SYNDROME

Free write about what you bring to the table that literally no one else does. Consider your past, your knowledge, your abilities, your education, your passions, your grit, your determination, your love for the brand and the idea – all the unique experiences that give you a unique approach and fingerprint that no one else has.

Be sure to brag about what a badass you are. Because every time you feel the imposter syndrome creep up you will pull out this piece of paper and read it to yourself as a reminder that you are doing the right thing and that you deserve to launch this idea.

EXERCISE: OVERCOMING BARRIERS

Write down a list of every single potential barrier you foresee facing in the launch of your idea. The barriers could be internal or they could be external. Then, next to each barrier, write down three ways to overcome those barriers. What obstacle will try to get in your way and what are three ways you can get past it, around it or over it? Hint: the free write exercise above is a great tool to get over internal obstacles. This is a phenomenal tool to keep you focused and moving past the stage of fear.

CHAPTER 03: BRAND YOURSELF BEFORE OTHERS BRAND YOU

"Your brand is what other people say about you when you're not in the room." – Jeff Bezos

REBRANDING THE WORD "BRAND"
"Branding is so much more than just a logo," according to Emily Soccorsy, the brand strategist and the co-founder of the branding company Root + River.

Conventional wisdom has taught us that your brand is your company name, logo, color palette and even your corporate slogan. This outdated definition has been reinforced by years of marketing and entrepreneurial courses.

"The brand is how other people experience what you believe," said Soccorsy. "Your brand is sprung from your beliefs, when you choose a purpose in life and when you understand what you want to do to bring value to the world."

Most of us were raised with the industrial mindset; we naturally separate our work and business from our personal life. But those divisions do not exist anymore. Thus the source of a brand is not a marketing mantra, but the human element behind why you do what you do.

"If you are not understanding why you do this, you will not be able to convey it to anyone else," Soccorsy said. "The only reason people will buy anything from you is because you believe in it."

People make purchasing decisions based on emotional reasons and it will happen faster than the blink of the eye. Once a decision is made, the brain will then pass that decision off to the left-brain to justify the decision already made with logical reasons. So we first buy emotionally and later justify logically. In order to make sales, you need to emotionally tap into and connect with your audience.

Or as Soccorsy said, "Every great brand is an invitation for people to believe what you believe."

WHAT IS THE WHY?
In order to determine your brand you must dig deep into the "why" behind what you do. Why are you choosing to do this work? Why are you here and why are you the only one who can do this?

This is not about your qualifications, but instead about your unique background and fingerprint that only you have. We have a tendency to focus on qualifications first, but nobody cares about that. They would much rather hear about what you believe in.

When asked about a purpose or a mission, many in the health and fitness industry will respond with, "I want to help people get better." That is a great response because we want to contribute to society as a human being – but it does not go deep enough.

"When you share what your brand is about, it should feel like the most important thing you've said all day. It should give you energy to talk about it," said Soccorsy.

If you have not gone deep enough in the exploration of the why behind your brand, if your whole body does not light up when you talk about your brand – there will be an obvious gap that your potential clients will see and feel.

The brand is the soul within your company. Thus everything you do, every project you put out, every client you take on, and every piece of marketing material you publish reinforces the root brand identity.

The brand is infused into what you call your business or project, what the logo looks like, what colors you decide to use and the mantra you identify with. Essentially all those things that conventional wisdom taught you was your brand are actually birthed from your brand.

All your future marketing collateral will be infused with your brand and your clients will connect with your brand in a way they could never connect with a business without a soul.

FOCUS YOUR VISION
"Vision becomes a filtering process. You will know what you need to do versus not do in work," said business architect and serial entrepreneur Mike Zeller.

Before you get too far into the launch of your branding it is important to create your guiding vision that will keep you focused for the work to come.

What is a guiding vision? I like to think of it as a set of non-negotiable principles and intentions that you can refer to for all future business decisions.

There are a multitude of business books that will give their own spin on recommendations for how to accomplish this – but my advice would be to find a few systems to homogenize together what truly works best for your purposes. After all, not one rubric or plan will work for everyone.

For the James Patrick Photography team it involves setting the following, which I call the 3 Ps: Purpose, Principles and Path.

Purpose: What is the reason I am going to do everything I do? There has to be a driver, a why, behind what we do.

Record that down because it will help determine what to invest your time into in the future and what to potentially avoid so as not wasting your time. If something does not align with your purpose, you know you can pass.

Principles: These are the guiding laws of not only my business but also for my life running this business. It is a lot of fun to look up what large brands set as their core principles and values to see what companies truly care about – and it might surprise you.

The five I've set for myself are to have fun in what I choose to do; to always be willing to dream, imagine and create; to provide unequivocal value to all our clients; that everyone on the team is accountable, including me; and, finally, don't be an asshole! The last one is the most important, obviously, because no one likes assholes. What are the guiding principles and laws you want to set for yourself? You might also enjoy revisiting this practice every few years and revising your value sheet. Ten years ago I would not have allowed myself to have as much fun and to dream as much as I do today.

Path: The path is all about where this is intended to go. Where do you want this idea to be in 10 years? What will happen in a decade? Setting the end of the path is important in being able to reverse engineer to see what you need to achieve in five years, in three years and by the end of this year. Using general numbers, your path could be to have $10 million in total revenue per year in 10 years. That means you need to grow $1 million in revenue every single year until then. Perhaps within 10 years you want to have had 100,000 people change their lives through your program. You could reverse engineer that to having the path of impacting 10,000 lives each year. Or perhaps you start with 1,000 a year for the first few years, then scale up after three years, and scale up again after five and so forth. The important part is to set a destination for you to focus on.

Momentum is preceded by clarity. So get super clear. If you want to push this even further you can add in a fourth P for promise. What is the promise your brand makes to your consumers?

EXERCISE: WRITE A FULL PAGE ADVERTISEMENT

Imagine that you know your mission, your purpose, principles, path and message. Now imagine taking out a full-page ad in a newspaper where you have to tell your story of how you got here and why you do this. Go through the practice of writing that story and really understanding it. Once you have that piece you can extrapolate from it and use it in a variety of ways and a multitude of content including social media posts, blog articles, your newsletter, video updates and more.

A ROSE BY ANY OTHER NAME MIGHT NOT GET PICKED

"A remarkable name for your organization, product or service is like pornography: It's hard to define, but you know it when you see it," wrote best-selling author and marketing guru Guy Kawasaki.

What to name your business or project either comes to you so effortlessly and easy that you are surprised it has not already been taken, or it will require you to sit and brainstorm and write a bunch of ideas on a white board as you pull your hair out trying to find the perfect match.

And there is a reason we put so much energy into what to call our brand. A name takes on an important meaning when it is associated with your company, brand or service. The name must be viewed with complete context.

Take the word "oxygen" for example. On its own it is the air we breathe. Combine it with the word "magazine" and you have a publication dedicated to helping women be the best and healthiest version of themselves.

The goal with naming your brand is to have a name that stands out and separates you from other brands while being clear enough to evoke an emotion and resonance with what you and your company stand for.

For the naming process, unless inspiration has already struck you, start by clearing your mind. After a few deep breaths get a solid stand on the intentions for your business. This is why you determine what the brand stands for first. Imagine the impact you want your business to have. Then, develop a list of 50 or so words that are associated with your brand and begin to play around with them.

As you write out your potential ideas, avoid names that are hard to pronounce, too complicated to remember, use unnecessary acronyms or are attached to a trend that will inevitably fade.

When you start to get closer on a few options, check out their availability by making sure no one else has used them by running searches through the USPTO.gov online database.

FLEX YOUR CREATIVE MUSCLE

Skip Wood is a cover model with a rich history of modeling for various magazines and acquiring different sponsorships. In 2017 he partnered with a few others to launch his own supplement company called Muscle With A Motor.

The brand was synonymous with his lifestyle of always trying different workouts and a love for outdoor lifestyle and activities. This was the type of individual he wanted to approach with his brand.

"Having a motor means you'll be able to keep going," Wood said. "We want to cater to people who can't wait to get home from work and then immediately rush out to go on an athletic adventure. These individuals have a good career but when the work day ends, their day is just getting started."

This is the life that Wood and his fiancé both live – further adding energy to the brand they are promoting. Once they get home from work they get out to the mountains to go hiking or biking or they head to the lake to go paddle boarding.

Does this mean that anyone who is not obsessed with outdoor adventures will not purchase his product? Absolutely not! That is the great thing about niching down your brand. You know exactly whom you are geared towards, but others will still seek you out.

Going further, the company developed the slogan "Fuel Your Fitness" playing on the idea of our body having a motor.

"Our goal was not just to fit in, but to stand out," Wood said.

This was achieved through the company logo and branding colors being blue, yellow and orange to help it stand out on shelves from other supplement products as well as through company led challenges and events that create a community around the product.

DETERMINE YOUR DIFFERENTIATORS

Each of us is so truly unique and we are each here for a different reason. There are things that you, and only you, can do better, faster, cheaper, differently.

These unique facets should be integrated in our company, not just at a product or service level, but at a branding level.

At James Patrick Photography our mantra is that we develop beyond the image. What does this mean? It means that any photographer, qualified enough, can make images that look really good. However my team has a proven track record of creating images that work. Our images get picked up for publications and get licensed for advertisements more than other photographers.

I personally can take that further as I have a background working in the media as a journalist, public speaker, podcast host, creative director and more. This bevy of experience truly means I am a storyteller. And as a storyteller, I have a wide array of mediums in which to craft and communicate my stories.

What are the unique differentiators you bring to the table that no one else does? What separates you? What makes you stand out?

This can be a bit of a scary practice to consider as during most of our upbringing we were encouraged not to try to be different, not to try and stand out. Instead we were conditioned to try and fit in, to not ripple the waters, to not be different.

However, in order for your brand to succeed like it deserves, you need to be willing to differentiate yourself. You need to be willing to contrast yourself from others as well as the audience you want to connect with. You have to be willing to be different.

Consider Southwest Airlines. There was once an idea that airline travel was too expensive for many people, meaning that only the very affluent could travel often. Southwest Airlines wanted to give almost all people the opportunity to travel. That unique differentiator was the founding idea of the company. That heart in their brand is incorporated into every piece of marketing they do.

"It is not a marketing tactic," said Soccorsy. "It is the root of the brand."

EXERCISE: MAKE A PROMISE YOU WILL KEEP

Successful brands in the 21st century deliver a promise to their consumers. Write out what your promise, or promises, to your audiences will be. They are non-negotiable, the things you will never waiver on regardless of the circumstances.

CHAPTER 04: BUSINESS FORMATION AND LEGWORK

"Amateurs sit and wait for inspiration, the rest of us just get up and go to work." – Stephen King

SETTING UP THE BUSINESS

The logistical formation of your business idea may seem like a scary step that perhaps has stopped you in the past, but it does not need to be. If you feel any hesitation or that fear start to creep up on you – then refer back to the chapter on fear and reread the affirmations and solutions you wrote to keep yourself moving forward.

Once again, you must ask yourself: Why are you really afraid? Are you afraid because doing these steps makes this idea seem more real, or is it because you've never done this before?

The reality is these are just technical steps that countless people have done before you. Many of those people are not as smart as you and certainly not as driven as you. The truth is that everything in this chapter and everything you will be facing can be figured out and can be achieved.

Realize that everything can be figured out. It is not like it was thirty years ago where it was so much more difficult to figure things out.

Don't know how to get a business license? Google "how to get a business license" in your area. Not sure how to file your taxes? Set up a meeting with a CPA to review your goals. Don't know how to set up your LLC? Go to LegalZoom or hire someone to do the paperwork for you. If you can't figure it out just hire someone who can. Then move forward.

When I launched my photo business I did not want to deal with the setting up the LLC, the taxes, business licensing and the like so I just hired someone to get it done quickly and correctly and I moved on with what I wanted to do. I did not let the fear of getting these tasks done derail me.

Your will to move forward with your idea needs to be stronger than the fear of doing the paperwork required to make it happen.

Do not fall into the trap at this stage of overthinking and overcomplicating things. Take quick action on these items and you'll immediately have a wave of relief wash over you. The act of starting something changes the perception of how hard that something appears. Psychologically you'll be primed for more and more action by taking these basic steps to set up your business.

Another thing to keep in mind is that the people who handle the filing of your applications or paperwork do not spend time emotionally thinking about what you are doing before they hit the approve button - so why should you put so much energy into worrying about it submitting your business license or registering for your tax id number?

Some of the following steps are not required for everyone – this chapter is written with broad brushstrokes to try to cover a lot of different business concepts. Some of these you may have already done. But here is a list, in no specific order, of things you should be looking into and considering whether it fits for you and the project you wish to launch. Do the legwork to figure things out now; there is really no later.

Determine Your Business Formation
Will you be a sole proprietor, LLC, corporation, partnership? Set that up. Have questions? Talk to a lawyer or even a CPA who has experience setting up businesses. Don't want to spend that much money? Go to LegalZoom.com or do it yourself.

Apply for Your Business License
Is a business license required for what you are doing in your city or state? Figure out if you need a license and fill out the required paperwork. Every municipality is different so just Google it or go to your local small business association website.

Determine Insurances You Need
Do you need liability insurance or any sort of professional business insurance for your business venture? Google it, figure it out and get the paperwork sent in for it.

Determine and Apply for Special Licenses

Are there any special licenses required for the business idea you have? For example, do you need to get a sales tax license to sell a product? Once again, quick online searches are your best friend to figure this out.

Set up a Business Bank Account and Credit Card

You will want to set up a business bank account and credit card that is separate from your personal accounts to keep funds apart from each other which makes your tax work and accounting or bookkeeping much easier and cleaner.

Set up a Way to Get Paid

What could be more important than getting paid for your business? Determine how you want clients to pay you, whether it is through PayPal, Stripe, Venmo or one of the many other merchant accounts. If you have a physical or online product you are selling, where will you be hosting the sales? For example, will you be using Shopify, GetDPD, Kajabi, AccessAlly etc.? Don't worry too much about picking the wrong option as you can always change it at anytime.

Set up a Way to Pay Yourself

Okay, this is now the second most important thing. You should be paid for your work! Set up a system to either pay yourself or regularly transfer money from your business account to your personal account. If you have questions about how much you should be paying yourself and the best methods in which to do so, set up a meeting with an accountant.

Set Aside Money for Taxes
Come tax season you do not want to be caught with no money in your business account to pay your taxes. You might be surprised to know this, but the IRS is not that forgiving of an agency. Weird, right? To avoid this, consistently make sure you are setting aside money to pay taxes. If you have any questions, once again, talk to a CPA. And don't be too angry about having to pay those taxes. Paying taxes is proof that you are succeeding!

Develop Your Contracts or Waivers
It does not matter how amazing you think your clients are going to be - you have to set up manners or methods in which to protect yourself. Set up contracts or waivers for your business. These do not need to be complex. Having a simple contract agreement is fine. Basically a document you and the client both agree to in what you will be doing and what they will be receiving. My first contract I set up was about a paragraph in length. Over the last 15 years it has grown to about two pages as I found new ways to protect my business. This is one of those things you figure out as you go, but you will want to start protecting yourself on your first sale.

Set up Your Invoicing System
Determine the system you will want to use for your accounting and invoicing. It could be QuickBooks or it could be one of the many online platforms now used. One of the best tips I can give you is to always be fast with your invoicing and keep clear records of when clients pay you and when clients are overdue. Don't expect clients to hunt you down to remind you that they owe you money.

Set up Your Accounting System and Budget

Set up a very simple accounting system and budget. To start, consider using the profit equation, which is very simply done by not spending more money than you make. Calculate all your projected profit which is the income you expect to make minus the expenses you anticipate having. Just use your best guesses on both. Consider costs like leases, insurance, supplies, marketing materials, photographers, designers, contractors, maintenance, license fees, rent, travel or accommodations, etc. Forecast your budget using very simple numbers and it will help you make better decisions on finances moving forward. This is something that I believe should be cast in Jell-O, not stone, meaning you flex and make it work with you in real time. If situations, expenses or income change – then just adjust your budget accordingly.

Set up a Dedicated Workspace (Not required but highly recommended)

Build a place where you go to do your business, even if it is just in your house. Perhaps it is a guest room you don't really use, or a den you can put a desk in. Psychologically it will feel different going into work versus just pulling a laptop onto your lap while you are still in bed wearing your PJs. Although you are still allowed to work in your PJs!

Assemble your Marketing Pieces

Purchase your domain name and hosting. Acquire all your social media handles (even the ones you don't plan on using). Basically put together the shopping list of all the tools and resources you may need to run your project. For example, do you need an account with Shopify? Do you need your website designed or updated? Do you need a merchant account with Stripe or Square? Do you need any special software or equipment to set up in your space? Do you need a logo? Do you need business cards? Make that list of everything you need and when you probably need it by. You might not be able to get it all now, which is totally fine, but at least it is all recorded.

BE CURIOUS AND GET FUCKING RESOURCEFUL

I truly believe that one of the most important assets an entrepreneur can have is curiosity. Over time we have been conditioned to lose or abandon our curiosity.

But being curious is about shaking off other's limiting beliefs, fears and cloudy lenses. So often we carry the fears of our parents, friends, employers – fears that are not ours and do not serve us. Let them go! Many great ideas fail because the wannabe entrepreneurs *"wantrepreneurs"* behind them are too afraid to get resourceful, look things up and ask questions.

This book is only one step. Connect with fellow entrepreneurs, small business owners, others within your industry. Don't be afraid to ask others smart questions. No one expects you to know all the answers when you are first starting out. When I launched my photography business, I sought out other photographers constantly to ask them questions.

I would ask on how they sourced locations to shoot at, their process for filing for permits, their needs for insurance, their recommendations for subcontractors, their input on how they tracked sales tax and even their process for bookkeeping.

Remove your ego from the equation. If you want to advance your business idea and gain momentum, you need to seek out and find answers for the questions you have in the formation and development of your brand.

Another great benefit of curiosity is that it is the leading element behind innovation. If you ask enough questions, eventually you will find gaps within your market place that you could potentially capitalize on.

Go into your business with childlike curiosity.

CHART OUT THE CUSTOMER EXPERIENCE
This is a helpful practice to ensure that there are not any gaps in your customer experience. To do this, pretend that you are a consumer who first comes across your product or service.

List out every single step, in order, that needs to be taken in order for the transaction to be completed.

For example, let's say you are selling an e-book. Your customer experience chart could look like the following:

1) See advertisement or promotion for the e-book on social media and go to website.
2) Land on sales page of website to learn about the e-book. They can click to purchase or click another button to learn more.
3) If they click to purchase they will enter their credit card information into your payment gateway application and the e-book will be emailed to them automatically through your digital file delivery program.

Upon looking at this you realize that you have the opportunity to upsell them at the third step right before they check out with an upsale.

Then you can secede to have their email address added to your autoresponder series after they purchase your e-book so over the next few weeks they receive maybe 7 more prewritten emails marketing another product or service for them to look into.

Charting out every step your customer needs to take can also shine light on any potential problems that customers could face such as being confused on how to purchase the e-book on the website or maybe they would be unclear how they receive the e-book once purchased.

EXERCISE: SCRIPT YOUR ACTION ITEM LIST

Write out all the things you need to get done and give yourself realistic, but strict, deadlines. Then applaud yourself as you are able to cross them off one-by-one!

EXERCISE: DEVELOP YOUR OWN RESOURCE LIST

Think about all the photographers, designers, web developers, accountants and marketers that you know. Supplement that list with other avenues such as your local small business association and any relevant professional trade organizations within your industry.

The rule to remember is that you will not get what you don't ask for. You have formed so many friendships, colleagues and connections over the years. Now it is time to ask them for something.

CHAPTER 05: FINDING THE ONE (CLIENT)

"Coming together is a beginning. Keeping together is progress. Working together is success." – Henry Ford

THE WHO

You don't put forth all this energy for no reason. You don't invest all this time for no one. So who is this all for? Who are you investing all your time, energy and emotion for?

You have already determined the why behind what you are doing and now it is time to determine the who. Specifically who is this for? Who is behind you getting up early or staying up late to grind out the hours?

It is important to be insanely specific about defining your client avatar.

Looking at market demographics and statistical measures are great but they only begin to scratch the surface of truly knowing who your client is.

You should know them in and out. What do they like, not like, what are their passions, what are their fears, what motivates them, what inspires them, what do they aspire to become?

Find someone who represents your ideal client and imagine being them for the day and go through each part of their day. Imagine you are them when they are waking up, making breakfast, checking their phone, heading into work. When does your product or service come across their attention? Free write a paragraph as soon as you finish this.

This comes down to whom are you trying to please. Does anyone else matter? I sincerely hope not because you should not be giving anyone else attention but your client avatar.

In fact you should be contrasting and polarizing who your brand is for and who it is not for. If you define that you can save time trying to chase down the wrong people.

Any business is far better having no clients than getting the wrong clients or bad clients.

Give your client avatar a name and an association. Think about how you will reach them and how you will convert them. Brainstorm how you will communicate with them.

A fear that might surface during this process is that you may be afraid you will turn people away if you are too specific in setting up your client avatar. That is totally fine. It is far better to niche yourself than to try to target everyone as we discussed earlier.

Focusing on one-person means that ultimately you will be able to serve more. There are a variety of exercises you could go through to strengthen your connection to this ideal client. You could imagine having coffee with them and what that conversation would sound like. You could write a letter to that one ideal person about how you plan to serve them and why you have started the brand you launched. You could find a stock photo of someone who looks like the client you are imagining.

This is all about launching to the right people.

HAVE SHARP EDGES
No one gives a crap about dish soap or laundry detergent. Why? Because dish soap and laundry detergent is made for everyone. It is generic in nature and as such it never gets discussed, never gets cared about, never has any emotions tied to it.

Contrast that to a car company. People typically are not passive about their cars; they often become obsessed by the identities they tie to their vehicles.

If you shave off the edges of your brand in hopes to appeal to more people, you will ultimately water it down and it will no longer appeal to anyone. It is all about being on the edges, the fringes.

Know with full clarity what you and your brand represents and who your clients are.

You want people to either say hell yes or hell no! That way you only need to worry about working with those who say hell yes and you can save the time trying to chase down people who say hell no!

A WEDDING RING OR A ONE-NIGHT STAND
Now let us shift gears into the two types of relationships you can have with your clients. The first is you can have a transactional relationship. The other is you could have a committed business relationship.

It is not dissimilar from the difference between a one-night stand and a marriage. One is focused on instant gratification without long-term commitment or benefit. The other is about the long-term play. It is about building trust, rapport and giving before asking.

Technically both can succeed, but only one puts the client in the center focus and answers the question of why you are doing this in altruistic fashion.

McDonald's probably cares more about one-night stands. They are focused on processing as many transactions as possible. It would be surprising to find a McDonald's who cares about developing long-term relationships with their customers. That is not say you will get bad customer service. But once the transaction is complete, they will be shifting their focus to the next transaction.

Now consider your favorite coffee shop you go to. I am sitting at one of my favorite ones now. I freaking love this place because the coffee is always consistently delicious, there is always spacious room to work, the temperature is always a great break from the Arizona heat, the music is chill and not distracting and the baristas are always pleasant. It won't be long before they have figured out my order by the time I walk up (since it is always the same).

Does it cost more to come here than to be at Starbucks? Absolutely. But I like the relationship here better.

My guess is if you are reading this, you are more concerned with great client relationships versus wanting to rush from one transaction to the next without ever caring for and about your clients.

SUCCESSFUL BUSINESS RELATIONSHIPS (AND PROBABLY PERSONAL ONES TOO)
The first thing is you have to know your clients, or your target clients. If they are similar to your avatar this should not be a hard step for you. You want to know about their wants and needs. You want to know about their habits and preferences.

For example, suppose you were targeting a magazine editor. You will want to know everything you can about that editors publishing schedule, the types of content they tend to feature, the service providers they tend to use and the goals they have with their publication and editorial direction.

Second is you have to demonstrate your expertise, your value, what you offer them that no one else can that will help them solve their problems, their issues, what they need help with. This is all in the marketing, which we will cover later in this book. This step in the client relationship process can go on indefinitely until they ask you to stop badgering them! Okay, I hope you are not stalking your potential clients. But maybe a few steps back from stalking to demonstrate your value to them.

The third step is when you get that opportunity to provide services to them you over-deliver. This is your chance to reinforce to them why you were the right choice. Seek out value-added benefits, and services that affirm their purchase decision was correct.

Fourth, and what most people fail to do, is you have to stay in touch. You must show them you are still committed to them even after the purchase is complete. You want to illustrate that this was not just a one-night-stand transaction. This was not just a hook up. You're in it for the long haul. You're the person who calls them the next day after the date.

HOW TO LOCATE PROSPECTS
Going back to the exercise of you imagining actually being your client as they go throughout their day – you will see what their day is like and all the various ways in which you could connect with them.

I call these touch points. What touch points are available for you to connect with your target audience? For example, do they listen to certain podcasts that you could be a guest or advertise on? Do they read certain publications you should be featured in? Do they follow certain social media channels you could collaborate with? Do they hang out at certain coffee shops you could post materials at? I write that as I look up at an advertisement for a local bakery. Their ad states, "Get baked… cookies." Sold!

Figuring out these touch points will be an instrumental component of determining your marketing plan later in this book.

THE FIRST ONE
We always will remember our first one. My first real freelance photography client was a small clothing boutique that opened in Tucson and needed help with creating photos for their online and print advertisement campaigns.

Getting your first client and resulting first sale changes how you look at and handle your business moving forward in a profound way.

"Everyone feels like they are going through a bit of an imposter syndrome before their first client," said fitness entrepreneur and online coach Karey Northington. "Why would anyone pay me for my expertise? But when you get that first paid client you receive all that validation that people are seeking for your expertise in that category. This is what I'm passionate about and people are wiling to pay for it!"

Your confidence skyrockets while your focus on the next step sharpens.

KEEP THEM COMING BACK FOR MORE
Believe it or not, it is actually not difficult to keep your clients happy and returning for more. Consider what makes you happy with the brands you purchase from.

The number one thing, above quality, above consistency – is great service and great service is a result of feeling like you are heard.

"The number one mistake I see is entrepreneurs not getting feedback from their clients," said Nortington. "How they can improve and progress the relationship even further."

All successful brands have a system in place where customers can provide the brand with feedback. The most innovate brands are finding ways to incorporate real time feedback and insights as implementation in their business.

Feedback can sometimes be seen as negative. You need to prepare yourself and be open to and appreciative of all the feedback you receive. How else will you know how to improve?

Remember the fourth step to a successful client relationship is staying in touch with your clients.

You will get so much repeat business by properly giving past clients their due attention. But even more, some of the best ideas I've ever had in my brands is by having great conversations with my clients after they hired me.

EXERCISE: WRITE YOUR CLIENT PROFILE
Give your ideal client more than just the basic demographic details. Give them an identity. Write it down in as much detail as you can. Know who all this work is for.

CHAPTER 06: MARKETING

"If you build it… you may still need Google AdWords." –
Jennifer Mesenbrink

MARKETING FOR DUMMIES (AND OUTDATED COMPANIES)

If you were sitting in a college classroom studying marketing right now, the professor might break down marketing into what is known as the 4 P's (not to be confused with my 3 P strategy for branding earlier). The four P's of marketing are:

- Price
- Product
- Place
- Promotion

Over the next few months in that college course you would dive into each in attempts to understand how to form your product, how to price it, where to place it in the marketplace and what promotions to run to increase sales.

Unfortunately in our highly interconnected society and economy, the 4 P's only scratch the surface of what you need to consider in your marketing efforts.

The entire fabric of the marketing landscape has changed drastically due to the impact the Internet has had upon our society. We have fundamentally shifted how we connect with others, how we seek out information and how we make purchases.

This new era has forced marketers to adapt to find new and more effective ways to connect with consumers. At the core, marketing is still about the spreading of ideas and although it has never been easier to spread ideas, it is now much harder to have those ideas leave an imprint on your intended audience.

If we were to place a name upon this new period in marketing and communication it would be the rise of the consumer. There is now an immensely vested power in the hands of those making the purchases that is unparalleled to anything before in history.

The consumer now has the power not only to decide, but also to make informed decisions. The consumer can now negotiate, research, review, as well as completely ignore any brand.

Expanding upon that last point, consumers have become cautious, weary and exhausted by advertising and marketing messages. There is a good reason for this. Advertisers have used and abused the attention of their audiences for decades and now consumers are fed up!

Now, consumers can, and will, actively block any and all unwanted marketing messages. Not only do I have caller ID on my phone to warn me about numbers calling me, but I can then go in and block numbers from known telemarketers and scammers.

Using my DVR I can skip right over commercials. My email service is kind enough to filter out just about any and all spam messages and if I don't happen to like what a sender is putting in front of me, there is nothing stopping me from flagging it as spam myself. I pay for Spotify to avoid hearing commercials. And I have paid for Hulu as well as YouTube Red to avoid having to see commercials when I want to queue up a video. I've even put my entire household on the Do Not Call Registry (little good it did sadly).

Why do I go to these extremes? I am not the only one! You are probably doing the exact same thing.

It is estimated that we are being exposed to up to 5,000 advertisements each and every single day. That is a new advertisement every 11.52 seconds! Back in the 1970s it was estimated we would see 500 ads per day. It has grown 10x in forty years.

Not just as consumers, but as human beings we are overwhelmed and weary of anything that smells of marketing and advertising.

Thus the old marketing strategy of only focusing on traditional campaigns such as print ads, social media ads, brochures, fliers, posters and the like is simply not enough.

Having these questions lead your marketing strategy can be a dangerous approach as it often leads to a never-ending money pit where you are constantly spending on collateral and half thought-out strategies without any overarching plan in hopes of showing a return.

THE BRAND KILLER

At the center of marketing and advertising are the questions of how you will reach your potential customers and once you reach them, how will you convert them into buying your product or service? And once you convert them, how will you retain them?

To rephrase those questions from a different angle, in your estimation, how many sales are you not making because customers can't figure out what you're offering and how it benefits them in just a few quick seconds? Remember the importance of describing your idea in a single sentence.

In our coaching programs we see our clients initially making two mistakes with their brands. The first is that they ask their potential customers to burn too many calories (pun intended) in trying to figure out what their offer is and how it benefits the customer.

The second is that they will focus on things that the customer does not care about at all. For example, trainers will focus on touting all their certifications and credentials when customers just want to know if you can help them lose weight.

Let me share a personal experience with you. I was looking to hire a new personal trainer. I asked some of my colleagues for referrals and was referred to three separate trainers. I contacted each one with information on what I was looking for and what I needed. Then I asked for their response regarding their availability, approach and price. One never got back to me at all. The other two could not give me an estimate of their price and kept saying, "It all depends." Not one of them got my business.

We live in a very noisy world. In this world, all of us are constantly bombarded by various messages from the second we wake up to the second we go to sleep at night.

Consider how many things are fighting to get our attention at every waking moment of our day. There is Facebook, Instagram, ads on Pandora, ads that come up before we watch a video on YouTube, TV commercials, radio spots, magazine ads, posters, billboards on the side of the road, bumper stickers, ads painted to the sides of buildings, e-mail, spam e-mail, SMS alerts, movie trailers; the list goes on and on and on.

And what is the result of all of this noise? We literally start to ignore and tune everything out. Our society has and is facing what we call an attention crash. We no longer care to pay attention to most things. Consider how many things noise has killed before they could blossom: innumerable ideas, products, services and non-profit campaigns.

The abundance of noise has murdered more great ideas and potential brands than taxes, the economy, competition and lawsuits could ever hope to.

What we think we are saying to our clients and what they might be hearing from us are two very separate things. If things are not made very clear and very quickly – we will not get the attention of our intended audiences.

In his book *Building a Story Brand*, author Donald Miller described it best when he wrote, "If you confuse, you'll lose."

WHAT IS YOUR SIGNAL?
What you should be focused on is your signal. In particular you will have to figure out the strength of your signal as well as the clarity of your signal.

At the heart of good strong signal is content. Content marketing has been the primary tool our clients, as well as countless other entrepreneurs, have been using to grow their brands.

It is about having authentic content that you offer to your audience that educates, inspires or entertains them. It has to be seen as valuable. Content is the new currency in the digital marketing landscape as it is the most trusted form of marketing.

The trend to have content as the cornerstone of a marketing strategy will only continue to get stronger, especially as younger generations become more and more savvy at avoiding marketing attempts.

Content marketing is focused on having consumers find you instead of you always having to find them.

Once upon a time there existed individuals known as gatekeepers. The job of the gatekeeper was to determine what qualified to be published and what did not. As an entrepreneur and business owner, your goal was to appease the mighty and all-powerful gatekeepers in hopes to get the story of your company published.

Oftentimes, that appeasement required spending an unparalleled amount of money in attempt to blanket the market with advertisements. Gatekeepers could exist because the number of media outlets was quite finite and there were no means, or at least affordable means, of self-publishing and producing content.

However, for the first time in history, the gatekeepers have been stripped of the power. Now, every single person has the power and ability to be their own publisher. This is such a crucial point that I don't think we spend nearly enough time recognizing or appreciating.

We have the ability to post something entirely on our own, to communicate, to spread our message without anyone's real ability to prevent, filter or even edit. This concept is both unparalleled and unmatched.

Our connected society has been the great equalizer putting all companies and individuals on the same playing field vying for people's attention. Big companies are now required to act like small businesses and entrepreneurs now have the leverage of a large corporation.

Of course big companies and brands can still do massive ad buys on social media and Google to outshine anything you could afford. However, with no budget at all, an individual could reach more people with their blog, their podcast, their Instagram post or their YouTube video.

Yet the double-edge sword is, of course, is that all of this contributes to all the aforementioned noise we have to deal with.

This is why it is essential to focus on the strength and quality of your signal.

SIX WORDS TO MOVE FORWARD WITH
A significant turning point in my journey came in the form of six words a vice president of a corporation I worked at shared with me. We were collaborating on a large dollar pursuit and were brainstorming ways to get our company's visibility and viability increased in the eyes of the client.

"It is not complicated," he started. "Be seen, be heard, be read."

As soon as he said those six words the sun broke through the clouds and cast a beam of light through the large conference room window to illuminate and form a halo around the VP. Okay, so not that dramatic – but it might as well have happened that way as I've carried those six words with me into nearly every brand I've worked to get off the ground.

Content marketing is about being seen, being heard and being read. It is about offering great resources, information, entertainment and value to an audience of our target clients. This is a far cheaper effort monetarily than pure advertising, but it does require the investment of time and creativity.

You are now a publisher. This means you have to think like a publisher. What topics does your target demographic care about? What does your client avatar want to know? What do they want to learn? What do they want to be inspired by? What would entertain them?

The mediums you choose to use with your content marketing are entirely up to you. Perhaps it is a written blog, a video series, 1-minute clips on Instagram, a podcast or an e-mail newsletter. Maybe you turn the new IGTV into your own platform of creating content for your audience.

To grow the amount of content you can create, consider developing pillar content. This means you develop a main topic and develop a variety of sub-articles or content around the main idea. This is also known as hub and spoke. You create your hub idea and spoke out other ideas from it.

You can also easily repurpose content by turning a video into a blog, pulling the audio for a podcast and capturing the best points for various social media posts. That is a wealth of content from a single video.

The key here is that most of the content you put out is to help your audience with something; it is not to sell. You have to create content that they want to see, not content you just want to do. With all the noise, people don't want to see another advertisement. They want to be informed, entertained or inspired.

I've easily written more than 1,000 blog articles and way less than 100 of them are asking for readers to purchase anything. Focus on adding more than ten times the value than you ever ask.

What are the ways in which you can be seen, be heard and be read?

MAKING DOORS
I am a huge proponent of blogging for a myriad of reasons. First, it is the best way to inform, entertain and inspire your audience on a regular basis, which is seen as a value you are offering for free. This gives your audience a reason to continue to come back to your website, which honestly is not a common destination for most to begin with.

Second, it creates a long tail content that is great for search engine optimization (SEO). This is an important detail to digest.

If I were to ask you what the front door to your website is what would you say? Chances are you would say your homepage. That is a common misconception. The front page of your website is any and every single page that a customer could land upon.

Everything page on your website is indexed by Google and that means every blog (which is a new page) is a new front door to your website that is separately indexed. Each time you post a new bog it is a new front door to your website. The more blogs you write over time the more front doors you create for your website. My own website still gets traffic from content that I created years ago.

If you continue this logic, you can now surmise that what you title your blogs is also pretty important as the title of your blogs are the titles that come up in a Google search.

If you were to title your blogs with the exact words and phrases your target demographic would be searching for online – you have a much higher chance of getting those clicks.

Think about the things you personally click when searching on Google. How do we search? We often search in the form of questions.

For example, what is the best way to… what does it mean when… how do I… best tips to… etc.

If we are naming our blogs or any of the content we are putting out in the same or a similar fashion we have a higher potential of people clicking our links.

And it is not exclusive to just blogs. The same principles apply to posting videos with show notes on your website as well as podcasts with descriptions.

The more content you create, the more opportunities you have to build a community around that content.

When creating an editorial schedule for your content, develop one that you can commit to – do not overexert yourself and think that you are going to be able to post a new blog five days a week. Admirable, but perhaps start with a blog a week and scale up from there. Set a calendar and write out a few entries to get ahead so you do not fall behind on posting content for your audience.

To save time on blogging, work in batches. Write a few articles at once and schedule their release on your site over time.

In efforts to further market your content, like blogs, make sure you are sharing the content across all your platforms to encourage traffic to go from your social media channels to engage with you on your website. Speaking of your website…

BUILDING A WEBSITE THAT WORKS

I truly care little about the esthetic look of a website, and I own a website design company! I care more about the purpose of the website and if it achieves that purpose. Your websites need to be easy to navigate so that the visitor knows exactly what is being offered and what they are being asked to do within just a few seconds of getting there.

Each page on your website should have some form of a call to action. The call to action is what you want people to do while they are on your website. For example your call to action could be:

- Click here to get started
- Click here if you are ready to take the next step
- Sign up for our free trial
- Sign up for your consultation

Never assume that people know what to do next on your website. You actually need to tell them. Everything needs to be spelled out.

The text, images and graphics you use all need to reinforce the direction you want people to take because you may only have 5 seconds or less to capture someone's attention.

As we discussed earlier, every page of your website is indexed separately by Google so the various pages you have truly matter. Each page should be about something unique. Google looks at each page individually and scans to see what it says it is about. So if one page is about a lot of things, Google will think it is not about any one of those things very strongly and rank it lower in searches. However if each page is about one thing and all the headers and text support that one thing, then it has a better chance of being ranked higher in searches.

When it comes to search engine optimization (SEO) there are both on page and off page factors.

For on page, Google very much cares about page titles, which is the title that appears in the address bar. After the page title, Google will then look to see what your H1 Heading is, which is the main headline on the page itself. From there it will look at what your body copy includes. Does the text on the page support the page title and H1?

Off page factors are essentially all about inbound links. These actually matter far more than what is on your page. How many other websites are linking to your webpage? Google wants other website to validate your web page by placing links directing people to it as a reputable place to go.

The process of building inbound links is an ongoing effort that you will probably do forever. The best way to do it is by creating good content that people will want to link to; yet another reason why blogging is so great. Other bloggers will want to link to it. You can further support this by putting social share buttons on your website and on your blogs making it easy for people to share your content to create more inbound links.

Simple rule of thumb: the more inbound links you create, the better traffic your website will get.

Now – let's shift gears to discuss how we can harness those people finding your content.

GETTING SOCIAL

If you want a secret and surefire way to grow your following fast, this is not the book for you. This book will instead focus on developing true fans. These are the people who will go on the journey with you. As you know, your brand is not for everyone. As Kevin Kelly writes, we only need about 1,000 true fans to succeed with our brand ideas.

When using social media understand that it is a terrible place to try to make your sales. Think about how you personally use social media. You don't use Facebook to go shopping and you don't have your credit card in hand when you get on Instagram. You're there to see stuff you want to see, to be entertained, potentially informed or inspired.

Thus this goes back to once again having great content that draws people in. Friends and family aside, consider the social media profiles you enjoy the most. Chances are they offer you something that you pull from. Maybe it is education, entertainment or inspiration. You pull something away from this page and that is why you follow them and have not unfollowed them or ignored them yet.

If social media is not for selling, what is it for? It is for that introduction. It is for the first handshake. It is for sharing great content. It is for providing great value to your audience. And finally, it is for inviting those true fans (once they become true fans) to take that next step.

What is the next step? Most likely it would be to visit your website for more.

For example, you could write at the end of a post:

"If you liked this, check out more on the new blog we just posted on our website."

"If you are hungry for more on this topic, check out the new video series we uploaded to our website."

"If you want to see the behind the scenes on how we made this happen, check out the new blog we just posted on our website."

It is a soft invitation to try to ascend a contact you've been introduced to on social media to take the next step in the journey to eventually paying you.

Also it is a smart technique to condition your audience to take action on every single post you do. The more they get used to taking action on every post, even if it just to like or comment, the more likely they are to take a bigger action such as going to your website.

Bear in mind that you cannot remove the social from social media. To get the best engagement out of your audience, conversations must be two-way and not exclusively you shouting from the top of your mountain.

When our team is promoting our FITposium conference, we are not exclusively talking about the event and why people should pay to attend. We are also connecting with our followers, engaging them on their channels, paying attention to what they are doing and getting involved in their conversations.

Taking those steps show authenticity and begins to create that brand engagement and loyalty.

It is far better to have 100 truly engaged fans than it is to build a passive audience of 10,000 who don't really pay attention.

Consider developing a social media calendar so you can plan out what content you want to share on what channel on what specific date. This keeps you focused and on track and also gives you a reference to look back to chart out what content works better as well as when it works best.

Wondering what the best platform is to be on for your brand? The answer is simply whatever platform your audience is on. You may find that your target audience is on Facebook and Instagram but not LinkedIn or Twitter. Or you may find success on YouTube and through a podcast on iTunes but not through Instagram. Test to find what works and always be prepared to pivot as new platforms launch and gain momentum.

NEVER EXCLUSIVELY RELY ON SOCIAL MEDIA
As much as you think you might, the reality is you do not own your social media following.

I feel quite sorry for all those people who wasted all that time and money trying to build a huge MySpace following. What is that worth now?

What will all those Facebook friends and followers be worth in 10 years?

Will Instagram followers be worth anything in that same time?

You do not, and will never, own any piece of the social media channel or those who connect with you on it. The channels will continue to evolve, disappear, launch, shift and change algorithms so we will be able to reach less and less of our audience.

Remember when a native post on Facebook could get you all the traffic you could ever hope for? Remember when nearly all of your Instagram followers saw your posts?

Now how many unpaid likes do you get on Facebook compared to your following?

It is no use getting mad at these companies for wanting you to pay more to reach others. That has precisely been the business model they established from the start; the same one that you willingly signed up for by providing all of your personal information to create an account for free.

If social media died right now, how would you reach anyone in your audience? About a few months before I wrote this chapter, the servers that held both Facebook and Instagram went down for a few hours one weekend morning impacting some users from different parts of the world. At our office we could not access either website or app for about two hours. My question to my team, albeit a rhetorical one, was to inquire what we would do if it never came back online.

Our companies would actually be just fine because we focus on what we do own. We own our e-mail lists. E-mail will be your most effective way to monetize the followers you have.

My focus is to use social media to entertain, inform and inspire my audience – slowly guide them to my website where they could sign up for my e-mail list and then I have the ability to truly market to them at any time.

This is the essence of the book *Permission Marketing* written by Seth Godin – which is still one of the best marketing books ever created.

When someone goes through the steps to sign up for your e-mail list they are giving you their permission to market to them. You are no longer spam. You are no longer noise. You have been granted permission to have their attention. And in today's society, there are very few things more important and valuable than the attention of others. And unlike social media, you actually own your e-mail list. And while social media and search engines consistently change their algorithms, there is no algorithm for e-mail. It is all about meritocracy. The better content you create, the more people will want to open your e-mails. The best content will always win.

For effective e-mail marketing efforts you will want to set up with an email service provider. There are numerous ones available such as MailChimp, Aweber, Constant Contact and more. The costs run from free to very expensive and the services run from minimal to vast. When in doubt, start with a free one and scale up if you need to.

In any e-mail marketing your subject line is extremely important. Your main metrics are your open rates, number of people who opened your email divided by the number who received the email as well as your click through rate, which is the number who clicked on a link in your email.

The simplest e-mail strategy you could offer is for subscribers to receive your blog articles, or podcasts, or newsletters sent to them instead of them having to go to your website whenever you do a new post.

Regardless of where you are at in your e-mail list, you want to start training your subscribers with every e-mail. One of the best ways to do this is to ask them to click on a link in every e-mail that is sent to them. The more they are conditioned to clicking on your links, the more they might be willing to click on a link that asks them to purchase something later down the road.

The more you do email marketing you will eventually start to develop multiple lists so you can communicate to each list separately. For example, you could segment your lists into current buyers and prospect targets. Thus each list could have a different series of autoresponders to either convert prospects into buyers or buyers into bigger buyers.

Autoresponders are a series of prewritten emails that are sent out to subscribers at timed intervals with the goal of ascending the subscriber further into knowing about your brand, what your offerings are and eventually asking them to make a purchase, or a higher level purchase.

But, at its core, e-mail marketing all comes back to offering great content. Having great content that you share to those who gave you permission builds trust and rapport with your target audience. It converts those on the sidelines to being true fans.

Quick note on the other end of permission marketing: people have the control to opt in to your messages, but they also have the control (legally) to opt out at any point.

If everyone is opting out of your list, then something is wrong in your messaging. But sporadic and occasional opt outs are actually a really good thing.

It is people saying, "You no longer need to waste any time, energy or money marketing towards me because I am out." You never need to worry about marketing to them again. Focus on those who are still in.

TURN ON THE HIGH POWERED MAGNET
One of the best ways to grow your e-mail list is to offer something extra in exchange for people's name and e-mail address. This is called inbound lead generation and your tool for this will be a lead magnet. Lead magnets could be in really any form you want – but it comes down to something of value that is essentially an appetizer to a main course you could sell them later on.

Some examples of a lead magnet could include:
- Short E-Book
- Free Guide
- Top 10 list
- Free Video Series
- Short E-Course
- Quizzes
- White Papers
- Case Studies
- Tip Sheets
- Video Demos
- Trend Reports
- Free Assessments
- Recipe List
- And more

The idea is a free resource where you can develop a pool of potential consumers to ascend through a series of offers. The individuals who take the journey from your social media channels to take action on your offer are saying to you that they are interested in more from you.

Focus on delivering the best value you possibly can. You must always give your best stuff so subscribers do not regret signing up for your offering, albeit free one. The idea is to build and nurture the list of potential customers and create a journey for them where you are growing both trust and likeability.

Anyone who obtains your lead magnet is a lead you must nurture to take the next step, which could be a small paid item as you ascend them up to hiring you and paying you for something bigger.

"Start with something small," Northington says. "It is very difficult for cold traffic to randomly convert into a big sale so you should be starting with small product. You can use freebies like blogs, photos, videos or PDFs to build that trust. From there you move them up to a paid item.

It is a lot like starting a relationship and the first date has boundaries. Your first sale is the same way."

Realize that people are not solely buying your product, service or commodity. They are buying feelings. They are buying you!

ENGAGING WORD OF MOUTH

Word of mouth marketing is truly as old as the human language itself. If you do really great work or provide a really great product, people will want to spread the word of what you do on your behalf. However you have to empower them to do so and equip them with the necessary resources to do so effectively.

Word of mouth marketing is giving people a reason to talk about your stuff and making it easy for that conversation to take place.

As we have established, the reality about marketing is that the consumer is in control. They have more information then ever before. It is not like it used to be when buyers had to beware of nefarious sellers. People review things like crazy and they also seek out the reviews of others.

A bad seller cannot pull the wool over the eyes of the consumer for long. You, as the amazing service provider you are, must focus on your consumer's experience – so much so that they are ready to rave about you.

If you were to sketch it out, every lead you nurtured who has become a consumer has followed the same process. It started with getting to know you, then to like you. From there trust was established, and then they decided to try and buy from you. After that they became a repeat customer. The last step is they want to refer you to others.

If you make your customers happy, they will become your best form of advertising. They are essentially doing the content marketing on your behalf.

Engage your consumers regularly to learn how you are doing. Fix what is broken and give them the opportunity to share what is working beautifully. The reality is they are already having conversations about you and your brand. The question is really if you are willing to join in on their conversation or not.

How can you encourage your audience to share their experiences working with you? The simplest way is to just ask them to. Ask them to write testimonials. Ask for permission to share their stories of working with you. Create share buttons on your websites so your audience can share your most valuable content. Have a forwarding option in your e-mail newsletter so they can push your content to their community. Consider having swag for your best customers to further promote you. You could even go as far as having a community of your top evangelists that you form, engage with and celebrate with. For example, with FITposium any of our past attendees take on the title of FITposium PRO and our team constantly seeks out exclusive opportunities for our PROs to level up their careers.

EXERCISE: CHART OUT YOUR MARKETING INITIATIVES

Spend some time to develop the various marketing systems you would like to employ, what will be required to manage each and what your goals are with each effort. Do not be afraid to get specific here. The only way you will be able to improve your marketing will be to test and measure the results. What gets measured can be improved!

CHAPTER 07: LET ME TELL YOU A STORY

*"Marketers didn't invent storytelling.
They just perfected it." – Seth Godin*

THE PRICE IS RIGHT

I am going to use your power of imagination. Take a moment to imagine a small toy car, the kind you buy in any convenience store in the world. The only details I can give you about the toy vehicle is that it is about two inches in length and is modeled after a Pontiac Trans Am. The brand of the toy is irrelevant in this game. Now, how much is this car worth? The retail is probably around $1.99 – but what is it worth? What is the value? Answer at the end of this chapter. Don't skip ahead!

WHAT'S YOUR STORY?

The essence of content marketing is all about storytelling. The components that make a great story are the exact same components that create a great life. Each of us is already living such a great story. But what we need to learn is how to tell that story better, faster and with greater impact. We need to learn how we can invite people into the story to get them involved with our brands.

"Stories are the most powerful way of sharing any message," Soccorsy said. "Brain activity between two people will sync up when one starts to tell a story."

The question we will focus on is, what is your story? The best part about your answer is that it is already right there. You have all the necessary pieces and elements of your story already. You just need to piece it together and share it with the world. How you do that is truly what makes the biggest difference.

People will not only pay attention to a great story – people will believe a great story. Not because it is necessarily factual, but because it connects and affirms with our own beliefs.

Storytelling is the oldest form of human communication. We have told each other stories to help us make clarity of the world around us. As such, stories wield immense power.

A great story can easily sell a product, but it can also elect a politician, start a movement, and create a tribe.

Once your idea is partnered with a great story, it can gain momentum and traction. An idea without a story, or a poor story, is more likely to die.

We have already addressed that the landscape of communication is entirely new and still being mapped out – yet stories are still being used as narrative shortcuts to help us sort through all the overwhelming data and noise. But even though the era has shifted, the fundamental elements of story such as plot, character and conflict all remain the same.

DEFINING STORY

It would seem that something that has been around as long as storytelling would be easy to define – but that is not necessarily the case. Even through we literally tell stories every single day of our life, it is difficult to distill down what a story is and how to apply it to our business.

A simple definition of a story is that it is a narrative about a character who is forced to deal with some sort of obstacle to try and achieve some goal. Pretty simple, right? Let's expand upon that into the three acts. Every story comes down to having a beginning, a middle and an end. This was popularly illustrated through Joseph Campbell's *The Hero's Journey*.

The first act, the beginning, is where you introduce the elements of the story such as your characters and what type of story this is going to be.

In the second act you introduce conflict and make things really hard for your character.

The third act is when your character emerges transformed.

You can see through this three-act structure how a character arc works. In a great story you start with a character (the hero) who your audience can relate to. Then you put that hero through really hard times as they are trying to achieve something great. That is something that every single person reading this can relate to.

How many times when you have been striving to achieve something have things gotten really difficult and you were forced to dig down deep to find the strength to overcome those obstacles? It has happened to each one of us. That is exactly why stories are so important. It is after you go through that where you and your hero emerge transformed.

FOUR ELEMENTS OF SUCCESSFUL STORY BRANDS

Every successful brand story includes four elements. The first is that the story is true. When I say "true" I don't mean factual. I touched on that a little already. By "true" I mean the story is consistent and authentic. Your brand cannot contradict itself because brands with authenticity are the ones to thrive. When there is a misalignment in what a brand promotes versus what it does, consumers will take notice. I'm certain you've seen that yourself when you are dumbfounded when a brand does something that does not seem in alignment with their core values.

Consumers are on the lookout for authenticity, and fake brands or brands that lack consistency will not hold up to scrutiny.

The second element is that the story must resonate with the audience. The best stories we hear don't necessarily teach us anything new. They tend to reinforce what we already believe.

This is why we buy books and magazines that confirm what we already think instead of challenging our beliefs. This is why both Fox News and CNN can co-exist for two entirely separate audiences. We do not like advertisements that are not for us, about us or interesting to us.

Thus, a brand's DNA; its core values and beliefs must sync and fall in line with the prospect. A great story tunes into the frequency of the audience; it does not require the audience to change their tune. My work as a sports photographer does not speak to or operate on the same frequency of that of, say, a pin up model or a culinary client or a homebuilder.

In early 2010 I was a project manager for a marketing and advertising campaign for the non-profit organization known as Voices Inc. This was a fantastic organization which set forth to mentor youths on the importance of story telling, setting in place the mantra of "your story is your power." The impact this organization had on the local community was critical. Not only was it a safe place for these kids to be between the hours of three and six every day, Voices was directly responsible for leading 75% of their youths to become first generation college graduates. It taught these kids the importance lessons of how to shape and communicate effective stories (what you are all learning right now). However the organization was maxed out and could not afford to accept any more applicants, and thus needed to increase its funding from donors.

Our project involved creating a direct mailer, which was to be sent out to our target audience from a master list of nearly 4,000 individuals. It is essential to note that this was a permission-based list of recipients who have either donated to Voices or volunteered at Voices or are familiar with the organization. Why is that important? It is critically important because these targeted individuals have already expressed that they share the same vision with the brand. They trust it – and trust is a scarce resource. No one succeeds in telling a story unless credibility has already been earned. The reason the campaign worked is because the stories resonated with the audience.

Facts alone are not as powerful as emotion. This is why client testimonials work so well. Testimonials are statistically insignificant data – yet they work psychologically because it appeals to our ethos, which we then support with our logos. Realize that we are humans first and consumers second. We will purchase for emotional reasons and later justify for rational reasons.

The third facet of a great story is that it is unique and different. A story that is different does not aim at everyone. If you water your story down to appeal to everyone, it will appeal to no one. Also, you will not succeed if you try to tell the same story your competition is.

So what if your niche is filled? Create a sub-niche, a spinoff, revise it, redefine it, differentiate it. Be the first in your new genre or category and find others that already want to be a part of it. You must sell something different by telling a different story.

The final element of a great story brand is that it makes a promise. That promise could be fun or money or wealth or health or happiness or safety or it could play off a consumer's fear. And to follow up on that, that promise… is kept.

In 2005, childhood friends Jeffrey Kaiserman and Stephan Ochoa opened an authentic Italian gelato shop in Arizona shortly after returning from a tour of Italy the previous year. It was the first of its kind in the state, and perhaps even the southwest. Jeff and Stephen truly believe that the finest tasting ice cream in the world is gelato and they would not take any short cuts in bringing this dessert to the desert.

This company itself is a great illustration of extraordinarily successful brand stories. Authentic Italian gelato. That is the promise they made to the consumer. They import all their raw ingredients from Italy and make it fresh, every single day. The gelato must be kept at a consistent temperature otherwise it loses its texture, which is integral to the experience of eating it. So Jeff and Stephen made sure their process for creating, flavoring and displaying the gelato was extremely precise. No corners were cut. They realized they might not make money, but it would help them grow over time. And grow they did. Two additional locations within a few years and a few years later they were franchising.

And how did Jeff and Stephen keep that promise? I know it wasn't smart to put up that image during a fitness conference, sorry. Jeff and Stephen were approached about wholesaling their product in grocery stores. This could have made them a tremendous amount of money immediately and aided them in quickly expanding their brand in multiple stories. But they declined. Why? Because with wholesaling you lose the ability to maintain quality control – which includes the precise temperature the gelato must be stored at. They lose that when the product is shipped and stored in stores around the country. This breaks the promise that FROST makes for fresh and authentic Italian gelato.

Want proof of a company that made this mistake? Look at what bankrupted Krispy Kreme's.

TELLING YOUR BRAND STORY
"People want to hear stories," Soccorsy said. "If you truly care about them, you will want to share a story with them."

As a brand you have so many stories you can share with your audience. You can share your own story and why you founded the brand. You can share the story of the evolution of the brand. You can share the obstacles you have overcome in the growth of your brand or the pivots you've had to make along the way.

You can further connect with clients by sharing the stories of success with clients you have had showing where they came from and where they ended up after working with you.

You can share the testimonial stories of your clients to help increase your resonance with your current prospects.

The idea is that you don't rely solely on facts, qualifications and statistics. You focus on the story of your brand and eventually the story of your clients.

You are an amazing storyteller and you have so many great stories you can start to share. Don't deny your audience that true connection.

A SIMPLE GIFT

I know most everyone thinks they have the best Grandma in the world, but I am going to say that I truly have the greatest Grandma in the world. A full-blooded Italian, evenings at Grandma's house were filled with lots of pasta and meatballs along with the most delicious Italian cookies you could imagine.

My best childhood memories at her house were Christmas Eve because that was the day that everyone went to Grandma's house for dinner, dessert and gifts. Grandma was not terribly wealthy living off her savings and my Grandfather's pension. Thus the gifts she got her grandkids were never extravagant. Every year she would fill a stocking with small trinkets she would find at the grocery or convenience store. A deck of Go Fish cards and some hard caramel chews were usual staples.

However one year she got my cousin and I something different. She bought us each a small toy car. Not that they were expensive, it was just that it was a gift she would not normally buy for us.

I remember that day my cousin and I racing our toy cars up and down the aisles of her house. As we were leaving, my parents, in their infinite wisdom, made me leave the car at her house so I would have something to play with the next time I went over there, which was often.

Well as most things go as a kid, I lost the toy car.

Two decades later I lost my Grandmother.

A woman so strong to have beaten cancer, twice, was taken at the hands of an aneurysm. She passed as peacefully and comfortable as she could lying in a hospital bed with her children by her side.

After her passing I was helping the family go through her possessions to determine what would get donated or given to family members. She had this extremely old couch that I would sleep on most nights when I stayed at her place.

We went to take it out to the dumpster and upon lifting it something fell out of the bottom of it.

A small toy car. A toy car that was given to me 20 years earlier. So I will now ask the same question I asked at the beginning of this chapter. How much is this car worth? To some, $1.99.

To me, it is priceless.

EXERCISE: WRITE YOUR STORY

Write out the story of your brand. Use the three-act structure presented in this chapter. Who is your hero? What complications did your hero face? How did your hero emerge transformed? Once you have it written out, practice telling that story over and over again.

CHAPTER 08: THE ART OF SELLING

"The are no cover bands in the Rock and Roll Hall of Fame." – Scott Ginsberg

THE NEW AGE OF SALES

How many times have you uttered the phrase, "I am not good at selling" to your friends, family, coworkers or colleagues? What a weird thing to say. You are no good at sales.

When you wake up every day and get ready what do you do? You wear an outfit that looks good on you, you style your hair to look appealing, hopefully you brush your teeth to save everyone from your bad breath. Is this not selling yourself to everyone you meet? Suppose you meet someone for the first time and you shake his or her hand to introduce yourself. In that moment you are now selling yourself. You want to ask your boss for a raise and guess what, you are selling yourself. When you are on a date you are selling yourself.

We sell ourselves all day long every day of our lives. But we don't like to look at it that way and somewhere along the way we got this bad impression of what sales is. When we think of a salesperson we imagine a cheesy middle-aged man in an oversized and poorly coordinated sports coat trying to get us to buy a lemon car or an unwanted telemarketer calling us to try and rob us of our money. We were raised to look out for crafty salespeople. That is how the phrase "buyer beware" became so prevalent in our lexicon. Yet it not longer holds as much truth as it once did.

In his book *To Sell is Human,* author Daniel H. Pink unmasks this old and outdated facade of what we think of with sales. We are all salespeople and selling can actually be as natural to us as breathing. And like with any muscle, the more we exercise it through training, the stronger it will get.

Today, the buyer now has more power than ever. As Pink illustrates in his book, our new economy is based on a new mode of "seller beware." Bad sellers need to beware of trying to cheat people or sell something they know to be of poor quality, reputation or accuracy.

Consumers are far savvier than they ever have been before and on top of that, they are very vocal about their experiences as shoppers.

Consider the last large purchase you made. Chances are that before you entered your credit card information, you pulled up a few reviews online to see what others, like you, felt about the product or service. I know for myself personally, checking Amazon reviews is a staple before I click that "Add to Cart" button.

If someone is selling a bad product or service, it won't be long before they are found out and exposed online.

The price of deception is far too high and thus the best sales people today are simply just the best people. They focus on the needs of their consumers and focus on delivering value first before asking for the sale. It is not about trying to make a single sale; it is about developing a lifetime relationship of sales with that consumer.

That is why people love giving their friends, people they trust, their business. Why hire a handyman you have never met before when you can hire someone you like and trust to do your work? Liking will always leads to trust and trust is the best opportunity for conversion. So if you want to be better at sales, then don't suck!

Quick suck test: Would you buy from yourself? If the answer is no, then you suck and you have to learn to stop sucking. If the answer is yes, then please continue reading.

CREATING YOUR OFFER
Thus far in this book you've developed your brand, determined who your target audience was and you've learned how you could be able to meet them by using social media. From there you learned how to court them through great content to head over to your website and sign up for your e-mail list so you can nurture from being a prospect into a client.

You have already stated who you are and what you do as well as set some expectations for what people can anticipate from you. Now is the moment you can make your offer to ask for the sale. And yes, you are required to ask for the sale. No one is going to give you his or her money without your offer and request.

As we discussed in the storytelling chapter, you cannot rely on being strictly-fact based in your copy. You want to focus on the client's emotional needs in purchasing. What would make them feel better? What would help them overcome their own struggles? Your customer is living their own story and this is where they have come across your brand. How will you help them get to their achievement? We have also addressed that purchasing decisions are made for emotional reasons and later supported with logic. These elements should be present in your offering.

Essentially you are selling what your product or service does for the client, not just what it specifically is. You need to stop looking at your offering as a commodity.

Your offer to your client should include a few major things.
1. The first is it must include a promise of how it will change their life.
2. The second is how it is different from anything else available.
3. The third is why they should take action now versus later.
4. And the fourth is the investment required to move forward.

Addressing those four things gives clarity to your audience very quickly.

When you are making your offer, it must be obvious how much you truly believe in your brand and how it can help the consumer.

Here is a sample offer from a completely made up company. "Knowing what to eat for your body can be so confusing! But not anymore! *Devour This* gives you the clarity you have been searching for to know what food is best for your specific body type! Unlike expensive cookie cutter plans, our 100% personalized and affordable meal plans help you to know exactly what you should be eating to lose weight and feel great fast! Don't waste another second, or another useless calorie trying to find the right meal for you. For only $19.99 a month we will make the exact meal plans you need to achieve your health goals!"

The promise is to help clear up the confusion of finding the right food for your specific body type. It differentiates itself by contrasting the personalization as well as the affordability. Immediacy is created by telling consumers not to waste another second (or calorie) on food that might not be in their best interest. Lastly it gives the price investment to move forward.

ENHANCING YOUR OFFERS
Just because the above offer played on having an affordable price, don't be fooled into thinking that you need to do the exact same thing. The more value you add for the consumer, the less relevant price becomes.

For example, part of your offer could even illustrate that your prices are higher because you have better service or better results than any of your competition. "Our prices are guaranteed to be more than our competitors, but so are our results with our large list of loyal clients who have returned to do more business with us 99% of the time!"

You could make your offers limited in time to create an additional sense of urgency for conversion.

Alternatively you could illustrate that benefits are constantly being added into your offering, so the earlier people purchase the more benefits they can experience. Your offer could include the line, "When do you want to start enjoying these benefits?" or, "Why deprive yourself of these benefits any longer than you need to?"

It is also crucially important to understand that the fear of potential loss is far greater than the desire for potential gain. Illustrating the loss people could feel by not taking action on your offer is a powerful sales tool. This is not about being deceptive in your sales copy – we addressed that. This is about finding a consumer's pain point and using that to help push the sale.

If you truly believe your product or service will benefit them, then is it not in their best interest to invest in your offering? If that means using pain point marketing, then so be it.

There are a variety of ways to introduce pain or the fear of loss into your offer. You could limit the number of units you have available, the number of days the price will be this low, or that others will have the benefit over them. You could have an offer that illustrates loss they will avoid such as, "Imagine how much money you will not have to spend in the future by doing this one time investment."

When selling our annual FITposium conference, ticket sales spike at three times. The first is when the tickets first go on sale because, "You cannot miss this." The second is right before the early bird price ends because, "Why pay more?" Finally, the last push is right before tickets sell out because, "Space is nearly gone and you might miss out!"

Just be careful not to be the boy who cried wolf. If consumers catch on that you are always pushing on pain points without any legitimacy behind it they are going to be additionally careful when purchasing from you in the future.

If your offering is tied to building a relationship with your client as opposed to a one-time transaction you can incorporate that into your offering. "I am not just selling you on this one item. I am selling a lifetime of commitment to you. I will be there every step of the way."

You will want to continually play with the copy of your offer to find what works best with keeping an eye on it over time, as copy that works today may need to be updated over time.

LEVEL UP YOUR SALES

There are some core elements that help lead to the best sales. As you are starting to learn, the best ideas are not necessarily the ones that sell. The best-communicated ideas are the ones that sell.

Authenticity in your brand is a crucial component for people to want to learn more about your offering. In the previous chapter on storytelling we reviewed the importance of having truth in your brand story. Truth is composed of having authenticity and consistency in what you and your brand represent.

This builds trust with your audience, which is another element that you should pay attention to. Your leads need to trust you before they ever are going to want to take the next step with you to become a consumer.

Creating familiarity is another strong way to level up your sales. This is achieved by being present and showing up where your prospective consumers already are. Participating in the groups they are a part of or being at the events they are attending. If the consumer forgets that you exist, that is your fault.

Often this trust is enhanced through the Law of Reciprocity. That is, you are giving to them great value before you are ever asking for the sale. This is why we spent so much time discussing content marketing and creating resources for your audience to find value in.

We have already addressed that your audience needs to actually like you to want to do business with you. The more likeable you are, the easier it will be for you to get work. See previous section on why you should not suck.

Another great way to level up your sales is to create a community around your brand. Brainstorm various ways to bring together your consumers as a tribe to share in an experience and journey together. The group should be distinguishable and have a culture so it is easy to know who is in and who is not. This creates a stronger sense of connection to the brand as a whole. Consider Corvette owners. They have the personalized plates, hats, jackets and meet ups all to celebrate how much they love the brand.

Spinning off of community, you can take your best consumers and use them as case studies in your marketing to illustrate and showcase social proof that your brand actually helps people.

Increasing value perception is one of the most effective means to increase your sales potential. Value perception is all about offering 10 times more value than you are asking for. If you are asking clients to spend $10,000 on your service, then you have to clearly show that you are providing $100,000 worth of value.

Consumers want to believe they are going to get their money back from their investment.

MAKE THE COMPETITION IRRELEVANT

The hardest time I've had in my photography career was early on when I tried doing the same work in the same market as others. I was neither unique nor different. It was when I got into fitness photography before anyone in my market did that I started to grow my brand as an artist.

Your goal is to separate and contrast yourself from your competition. There is far more potential for success by positioning yourself over your competition rather than being synonymous with them.

However, when you start to get successful, you will get more competition. Increased market competition is just part of any business. Your job is to always find new and innovative ways to differentiate yourself.

When an industry becomes overcrowded, it gets more difficult to differentiate your brand. Now that the market for general fitness photography is getting a bit congested I am making a few shifts and pivots in the work I am doing as well as the services I am offering to my clients to stay unique and different.

If you have not yet, check out the book *Blue Ocean Strategy*. It will guide and challenge you and your brand to break out of the red ocean of bloody competition by creating your own market space that makes the competition irrelevant.

Overall, what is required is you going back to your brand guide, knowing your true mission and purpose and what you are here to do that no one else can. That could be your unique selling proposition (USP), the guarantee you offer your customers, new market opportunities you come up with or a proven process or systematic approach that no one else uses.

In truth I was hesitant to put a section in the book on competition because I do not advocate entrepreneurs spending too much time worrying about competition. If you have done your research enough to know your brand is different, then focus more on your consumers.

Also I do not like to think that we live in a zero-sum world. I don't believe that in order for you to win, someone else has to then lose. There is truly so much work to go around. I would rather be in a position mentally of finding great work with great clients instead of stressing over what others who might be competing against me are attempting to do.

If anything, I actually thrive off my best competition. The best competition I have in my market forces me to stay on my toes. They push me to do better work. They encourage me to raise the bar. The reason is because I do the same for them. And the better one of us does, the more potential all of us have to grow.

Your end goal needs to be seeking to always adding value to the lives of your consumers and audience.

"To launch and maintain a successful business, you need to always make your clients feel better than your competitor does," said Mike Michalowicz.

You do this and you will create evangelists – consumers who will do practically anything to support the future of your brand. Any great entrepreneur knows who their true evangelists are. With great evangelists, who cares about competition?

TAKE CARE OF YOUR CLIENTS

A great way to be consistent with taking care of your clients is to do temperature checks with them. You could e-mail or call up your top clients to ask them how you could get a better sense of how to serve them. This should not be done as a sales call but a genuine attempt to do research on how to better your services.

We have already addressed the impact of word of mouth marketing. Checking in with your clients is not only a great opportunity to grow your connection with them but it is crucial to showing your commitment to them, which even though it was not a sales pitch, will help lead to reoccurring sales.

Any business will be vastly more successful by building reoccurring sales versus trying to always get new sales from new clients. Once you have a successful established relationship with a client, why would you not want to foster that and grow it to its full potential?

The top percentage of your clients will provide the massive percentage of your revenue. Thus you should never be spending your best hours on low hanging or low revenue clients.

Focus on your best clients that you can serve with the highest ability. You need to be asking what the lifetime value is of each of those top clients. Also, how can you increase the retention rate of those clients? Finally, are there leaks in your current system that you could be losing clients in that could be fixed?

What is required to do this? You actually have to care! You actually are required to give a crap about your clients and the work you are doing for them.

Having great relationships with your consumers is a great resource for your future marketing messages. You can and should be asking your best clients why they decided to choose you over other service providers. You could also ask clients you trust how they would advertise you if they could control the message. This feedback is great to know what works well for your brand and what could be implemented moving forward.

DOING AN INTERNAL ASSESSMENT
I don't like there being a single year that goes by without doing a SWOT Analysis for our brands. The process is quite simple and extremely informative and revealing to help you work on maintaining and improving the equity of your brand.

You start by listing out all the strengths you and your brand have internally. From there you then list out all the weaknesses, once again from an internal standpoint. After that I like to skip "O" for opportunities and move onto "T" for threats. This is where we shift to external factors. Externally what threats does the brand face? Once I have those three sections completed I shift to the opportunities. As with threats, opportunities deal with external factors. But the reason I save it last is because it is important to take into account the other three sections to see opportunities you could have with your brand.

It is truly amazing to look back at all the SWOTs I have done for the brands I manage over the years and all the great ideas that have been developed by saving the opportunity section for last.

OPTIMIZING ONLINE SALES

Driving sales through a website is a large goal for many entrepreneurs in any space, not just fitness.

First it is important to understand the difference between earned traffic and paid traffic.

Earned traffic is people who visit your website because they saw something interesting they wanted to explore further on your website. For example, they came across one of your blogs through a search on Google and jumped to your website to read it. Perhaps they saw the work you were posting on social media and decided to take the next step to explore your site.

Paid traffic is, as you would guess, traffic that you paid to see your site. This is placing an advertisement on Facebook, Instagram, YouTube or Google to entice viewers with an offer to head over to your website.

Generative earned traffic is important not only to improve your overall website rankings, but it also is essential in supporting your paid traffic.

If you plan on doing retargeting advertisements, which you probably should, the more traffic you can get to your website the more your pixel matures and can find similar audiences. What is retargeting? That is sending ads to those who have already visited your website. Ever notice when you check out a website you then start seeing ads for that same site on other sites you go to like Facebook or Instagram? That is retargeting and it is actually quite easy to implement and set up.

When you set up your retargeting pixel on your website you will then want to go into your Facebook Business Manager to upload your current e-mail list so Facebook can start to create a look-a-like audience profile.

When you are doing paid traffic to your site, you do not want to send them to your home page. Instead, send paid traffic to a specific landing page with an easy to understand call to action. This could be your lead magnet page with a free guide that you promote in your advertisements. This gets viewers into your funnel that you can them market with your e-mail sequencing to move to your paid offer.

If and when you start directing traffic to a sales page (or splash page) there are some key elements you will want to include to increase your potential for conversion.

You want to highlight the benefits of the features you are offering. A great way to do this is through video next to an attention-grabbing headline such as, "Make 6 Figures in the Next 90 Days!"

The video would be of you, or a voiceover, describing the entire offering, why it is important, who it is for, why people should take action now, what they could lose if they don't, how many this program has helped previously, what value added benefits there are and having a call to action for people to take the next step.

On the page itself there should be multiple clickable buttons as one goes down the page asking them to make the purchase. The buttons could say things like:
- I am ready for results now!
- I'm convinced, let's do this!
- I don't need to hear any more, let's change my life!

The page should have sections on the overview of the product or service you are selling and everything the buyer can expect to receive. It should showcase a section on the results others have achieved with the program including their testimonials. It can include a section of who the specific audience is to assure viewers they are in the right place. It should have a section on all the value added items the offering includes. The page can even include a section to thwart any objections that people might say to themselves in their head. At the end of the page it can also include a guarantee to build trust with the audience.

HOW TO SELL WITH E-MAIL SEQUENCING
Suppose you have your website set up with your lead magnet to encourage people to join your e-mail list. But what do you do once they subscribe to your list? You could just be sending them your weekly blogs, which is a decent way to increase their familiarity with you.

However setting up an email sequence, a series of emails that are automated to send out to the newly subscribed prospect, is a fantastic way to acclimate them and guide them to a sale.

The short end of e-mail sequences, or autoresponders, are about five to seven different e-mails that are sent out at predetermined intervals after someone subscribes to the list. On the higher end, email sequencing can go upwards of 30 or more e-mails.

Regardless of how many e-mails are included in the sequence, they typically follow the same path to ascend a prospect into becoming a client.

If you are launching a new product or service you want to sell, then all of the e-mails can be grouped into three major sections.

It begins with your pre-launch e-mails. Here you will want to show the various opportunities that are forthcoming to generate excitement from your list. You could send out e-mails that solicit input on your upcoming launch, which gives individuals a sense of ownership and investment in your product. You even have the opportunity during this time to showcase case studies such as client transformations and testimonials to enhance your resonance with your list.

Once you have launched your product you then focus on e-mails with the direct call to action to head over to your sales page to purchase. You can use elements such as limited time or price or bonuses to increase engagement and click through rates.

After someone makes a purchase you can continue to send them e-mail sequences to give them additional follow up information to increase value adds with your clients as well as to give them potential next steps to sell them on the next product in your offering, which should be of higher price and value.

For example if your first sale was for an e-book, your second sale could be for a coaching and on up and up until you are doing a high-ticket sale item. Clients don't necessarily buy your most expensive offering first. They have to be worked up that ladder.

EFFECTIVE COPYWRITING MADE SIMPLE

There are copious books on how to craft compelling copy that converts traffic into clients. I highly recommend you check out a few for your own edification. However to surmise a lot of what I've learned on effective copy, it comes down to focuses on three key elements.

The first is it shows that you have a clear understanding of who the audience is. You know about them and their wants and needs.

The second is that it hits on the problem that the audience is having in specific detail to further enhance the resonance the audience has with your brand.

The third and final is that it hits on the aforementioned pain points of what would happen if the audience did not move forward in marketing messages. The cost to not get involved should be so high that it is a no-brainer to move forward.

Your goal with your copy is to illustrate the prospect's life as it is right now and then their aspirational life they hope to achieve that your product or service can help them obtain. That contrast is where the best storytelling occurs – see the chapter on storytelling.

DEVELOPING YOUR SALES STRATEGY

"You always have to be marketing," said gym owner, personal trainer and entrepreneur Dave Dreas. "Marketing is the lifeblood of your business to always be bringing new people in."

One of Dave's sales strategies for his gym includes running evergreen ads on Facebook to direct traffic to a lead page where they will watch a video promoting a sale on a two-week training offer. Once the two weeks are up the clients are upsold to different programs. During this he is also running awareness ads targeting those who are within a half-mile of his location. His goal is to strive to have as many touches as he can so he consistently is dripping out content and advertisements.

"It actually may take up to 6-to-10 touches before someone actually notices your content," Dave said.

You can begin to see how Dave has mapped out the flow and journey his prospects could take before they become clients.

Karey Northington has a similar strategy for her online training.

"Facebook advertising has been my number one strategy," she said. "I am able to track and see who is interested and who is responding. I am driving traffic to my website through blogs. From this I can easily get a feel for who is interested in my content. I then use free lead magnets to get people subscribed to my e-mail lists where I can target that audience further."

Dreas uses e-mail as one of his main tools for client retention and acclimation. "I try to send out a few emails a week to the list I have for the gym. They will include tips and things to continue to help them with their fat loss or free workouts." He also manages a private Facebook group for all of his members to keep them connected and informed. He recently started doing a feature member of the month awarding them with a gift card to increase the sense of community.

Regardless if you are promoting a physical location or product or selling exclusively online, the key is systemization. There are various programs that allow you to drip feed out content. For example, each week you could distribute new workout videos and allow your members or subscribers only to have access to them.

You will want to be able to batch and pre-set everything so it flows with you simply monitoring it to make sure it works effectively and tweak as necessary. This means doing most of the work up front.

"They beauty of running your sales online is the low overhead," Northington said. "But you have to be careful what you are spending and invest smart. As you get leads, spend the time to follow up with them to show that you care. That simple act of caring will increase your sales."

EXERCISE: HOW TO MAKE SIGNIFICANTLY MORE SALES

Are you interested in taking your business to a new level with the number of sales you are bringing in, particularly if you have a higher dollar item or service? There is a simple solution that seems so obvious – but you might not be doing it as much as you should.

Pick up the phone. The more you are actually talking to prospective customers, the more sales you can make. Start making calls, start offering value and then ask for a sale. The more calls you make, the more comfortable you will get with the call and the more sales you will make.

Do not make the mistake of hiding behind your online marketing funnels. Personally connect with your audience if you want to convert more of them into consumers.

Write out your main talking points and answers to questions you anticipate before making the calls to help guide you through. In a short time it will feel much easier.

CHAPTER 09: GOOD, BAD AND UGLY REALITY OF PRESS

"Some are born great, some achieve greatness and some hire public relations officers." – Daniel J. Boorstin

HOW PUBLICITY HELPS YOU

The number one question I am posed with is, "How can I get published?"

If only there was someone who wrote an entire book on how to get published in the fitness industry. That person would be a brave, intelligent and dare we say a hero of the people! And if only this person titled the book "Fit Model Guide: How to Get Published" and made it available online.

I would certainly buy it, wouldn't you?

Okay, shameless self plug aside, the big misconception about getting published is that being featured in a magazine is the ultimate end goal.

I had a client who I helped get on two national magazine covers and maybe a half a dozen interior features. About a year or so later she was out of business.

How is that possible you ask? Because she did not leverage it. She looked at the magazine feature as the end goal and never did anything else to capitalize on it and the momentum she could have gained from it eventually dissipated.

Publicity is not the end goal. Publicity is a tool to help you achieve your end goal; which is however you define success for yourself and your brand.

Being featured in the magazine is a phenomenal way to increase awareness of your brand, quickly grow your audience, create third party validation for you, increase your sales and expose you and what you're doing in the largest platforms possible.

And it is not just magazines and newspapers any longer. I've had tremendous success in doing publicity tours with television shows, radio shows and lately lots of podcasts, which has been exponentially growing my brand's visibility.

If you want to work with the media to help grow your brand then you are in luck! The good news is that editors, hosts and journalists are always looking for great story ideas and content to feature. They need great contributors and it has never been easier to reach out to them.

The bad news is that it is super easy to get lost in a sea of crappy pitches from others, but certainly not you! The mission of this capture is to teach you how to get your pitches to stand out and then once you get press, how to leverage that press effectively to grow your business.

RESEARCH

The first step in order to get press is to do your research. What media opportunities presently exist in the marketplace that aligns with what you are trying to do? The goal is not just to have any press; it is to have the right press.

What outlets exist that share the goals, brand direction and audience with you? This is not about a shotgun approach. Pitching to the media is about being targeted and precise.

About once every a month or so I head over to the bookstore to see what magazines are on shelves. I look at local, national and international magazines. I see what content they are publishing, how often they are publishing, what the look and feel of the magazine is, who the editors are and even get a sense of their preferences. The same process can be applied to other forms of media like podcasts. I select the ones that are closest to communicating with the audience I want to reach and I explore them further.

I find out who the best decision maker is for the outlet. Is it the magazine editor or podcast host, or do they have a producer? Is there a section editor I should touch base with directly or can I go straight up to the lead editor?

For magazines I will even go to their website and download their media kit to see what their editorial calendar is for the year to see what they will be focused on in each issue that year. This is a great way to see if I can develop content that resonates with a specific issue they are compiling.

I put together a list of the media outlets I am trying to form a relationship with, along with the person I am looking to connect with, their contact information as well as any specific notes I can reference to help me later on with my pitches.

The fun part, if you want to look at it that way, is that research on press is something you get to do the rest of your career. People switch jobs, get promoted and move around. Magazines open, close and sell.

Realize, however, that media is great but not all media is created equal. It does you very little good to spend the time and energy to obtain media that does not sync with what your brand goals are.

For example if you are working to target women who are looking to improve their health and wellness, then targeting men's interest publications would not be in your own best interest.

Do not overlook the power of local media as well. This could be one of your best outlets for press and connection to a local audience that would be easy to convert into clients.

PITCH

After you've done your research on a media outlet you can comprise your pitch to them. An effective pitch is short and to the point and illustrative of a few key elements. You want to quickly highlight who you are and what you want to offer to the media outlet.

That is right, you have to show value to them. Why should they run a feature on you? What are you offering to their readers or listeners?

For example you could write, "My name is James Patrick (actually don't use that name) and I am a certified personal trainer in Arizona specializing in rehabbing injuries that many runners suffer from. I see in four months you are doing an issue on running and I would like to contribute an article to your readers on the top ways to stay healthy when training for a run. Attached are some of my credentials as well as a few images for your review. Thank you for your time and consideration."

Don't get too hung up on formatting. Just focus on showing value as quickly as possible in your pitch.

With the images you send in with your pitch, ensure they are images that are similar to what the publication would be featuring. For example, don't send sexy swimwear images to a women's interest magazine as it shows you were not paying attention to what their brand is. Make it look like you did your homework. Editors like that!

There are more things not to do than to do. For example, don't send one e-mail to a bunch of editors at once and put them in the BCC field. Don't misspell the editor's or the magazine's name. Don't write too long of a pitch. Don't have typos in your pitch. Don't send a pitch unless you've done your homework.

Also realize that it can take a lot of pitches before an editor takes notice. I've pitched clients, literally, for years before I earned the right to have their attention. Sounds frustrating and at times it can be. But focus on the bigger goal of offering value. Eventually they will take notice.

Follow up is essential when pitching. Just don't do it so often that it comes off as desperate or harassing. No magic rule here, just have to use your common sense. I would say absolutely no more than once a month. If it is less, that is okay as well.

You can also create a media kit to help in your pitch efforts. A media kit is typically a well-designed PDF booklet, which includes information about you, some photos, your credentials and anything you can brag about.

Also, don't limit your pitches to only e-mails. You can pitch through face-to-face meetings, phone calls and even regular mail. How you choose to share your work and pitch yourself is an art form in itself.

CRUSH OPPORTUNITIES

Once you get an opportunity to do a feature for magazine or be a guest on a show, then your next mission is to absolutely, without question, kill it. Reinforce exactly why they decided to take a chance on working with you.

Turn your content in early, make it better than they could have hoped for, hit all their specifications and requirements and perhaps even add in a few bonus value-added items to make it even better.

You want that person to know they made the right decision when it came to doing a feature on what you are doing.

Once again, make it more about them and helping them achieve their goals.

STAY CONNECTED
After a feature is completed, stay in touch with that contact person who gave you the opportunity. Chances are there will be more opportunities in the pipeline you could work with them on. Particularly if you did a great job for them the first time around, they are going to be more inclined not only to give you more work, but also to give you bigger work opportunities.

The biggest mistake one could make is treating a magazine editor as a one-and-done. It makes them feel used and like they were tricked into running a feature on you.

However, if you stay in touch and show your commitment to them over time you are going to find so many more opportunities to get your brand out in front of their audiences.

And as we already know, having repetition is important for any marketing campaign. Press features work the exact same way. The more often you are featured in the media, the more potential you have to gain the audience from that media outlet.

LEVERAGING MEDIA FEATURES

How can you ensure you garner the attention of those potential new viewers? Once a media feature comes out, it is more than likely the readers of that magazine or listeners of that podcast will look into you.

You will want to make sure all your social media channels are set up to direct the new traffic to take that next step with you, which more than likely will be to go to a landing page on your website.

Once they are on your website, there needs to be a very clear call to action for what you want them to do next. For example, it could be to get your free lead magnet or sign up for your free newsletter so you can start to target them with your content for the opportunity to sell them later.

You should be doing as much promotion of your media feature as possible, posting about it on social media, asking others to tag you in their posts if they saw or heard it. You want to create buzz around your buzz. This further enhances your validity as a credible source for people to look into. It also lets your audience know that this magazine or media outlet trusted you enough to put their name behind you, which increases resonance.

A publication is only on newsstands for about 30 days and most podcasts are only "new" for about a week on average. Those are relatively short windows to try to capitalize on their attention, but it certainly can be done.

You can further leverage media features in perpetuity by showing a listing of the logos of all media outlets that have featured you on your website and in your marketing materials as a fantastic way to gain instant credibility with visitors.

In addition you can post a section on your website showing all the press you have received for the same result. You can also go back to repost older media features as a way to show new followers or visitors the great press you have earned.

Also, past press is a great marketing tool to garner new press features.

EXERCISE: DEVELOP YOUR MEDIA TRACKING TOOL
Create a document, perhaps an Excel file, where you track the various media outlets you are working to develop a relationship with. Include their names, contact information and place notes for each time you send something out to them. This way you can effectively monitor how often you are in touch and can even see what they respond to more.

EXERCISE: CREATE A MEDIA OR PRESS KIT
Consider creating a multi-page PDF (or even printed document) that you can submit to the press that fully encapsulates everything they need to know about you in a single piece of collateral. The media kit can have a nicely designed cover, an introductory or bio page, your relevant resume (of other published features) and more. Putting time and energy into this shows that you take yourself and your brand seriously.

CHAPTER 10: NEXT STEPS

"We are what we repeatedly do. Excellence, therefore, is not an act but a habit." – Aristotle

As I wrap up the writing of this guide I am sitting in my favorite local coffee shop sipping away at my fourth cappuccino of the day. As I look at my watch I realize that I've been here close to 8 hours today alone concluding this project that was a full year in the making.

Why would I spend so much time on this project writing, interviewing and rewriting? Because it is my mission to provide you with the essential tools and information you need to push forward and excel in your career.

But, as with all my other pieces of work, in order for me to consider this book a success there is something else that needs to occur, and it will not be measured in the number of units I sell.

The success of this guide will be based solely upon what you personally do with the knowledge. It will be measured by the number of individuals who decide to push past that fear and make the decision to succeed.

If you put this book to use, please share the results of your efforts with me. I could not look forward to your success more!

Thank you for allowing me the space to be a part of your journey!

BONUS SECTION: RESOURCE LIST

MORE INFORMATION
FITposium Conference – Details at FITposium.com

The FITposium Podcast – Available on iTunes, Stitcher Google Play Music and FITposium.com

Fit Model Guide: How to Get Published – Available at FITposium.com (Click Store)

Four Steps to Effective Relationships (Free E-Book) – Available at FITposium.com

James Patrick Photography Blog – Available at JamesPatrick.com

Beyond the Image Podcast – Available on iTunes and JamesPatrick.com

PROFESSIONAL SERVICES
Photography: James Patrick Photography – JamesPatrick.com

Graphic & Web Design: Patrick Creative Media – PatrickCreativeMedia.com

Business Coaching & Consulting: James Patrick – JamesPatrick.com

CONNECT WITH ME
Website: JamesPatrick.com
Instagram: @JPatrickPhoto
Facebook.com/JamesPatrickPhotography

ACKNOWLEDGEMENTS

I am eternally grateful to my friends, family and colleagues who have supported me through my journey. It is because of them that I could create this for you!

The most massive of thanks goes out to my (soon to be) wife Kelly for supporting all of my crazy ideas, to my editor Carly for making my gibberish make sense, to my production manager Amber for making my businesses run much smoother and to my sister Kristina for all of her brilliant design work.

Also a huge vote of appreciation goes out to all those I was able to speak to in the creation of this book including Karey, Lindsey, Dave, Skip, Emily and Mike. Thank you for sharing your wisdom and always serving others!

Finally, in no particular order, it is important that I mention my mentors Bill, John, Alice, Tom and, of course, my parents for their guidance.

I appreciate you all!

Made in the USA
San Bernardino, CA
23 June 2019